The Funniest People in Television and Radio: 250 Anecdotes

David Bruce

Published by David Bruce, 2022.

THE FUNNIEST PEOPLE IN TELEVISION AND RADIO: 250 ANECDOTES

First edition. September 6, 2022.

ISBN: 979-8215088449

Written by David Bruce.

Table of Contents

Chapter 1: From Actors to Autographs 1
Chapter 2: From Bathrooms to Education 13
Chapter 4: From Live Television to Prejudice 38
Chapter 5: From Problem-Solving to Writers 52
Appendix A: Bibliography 65
Appendix B: About the Author 72
Appendix C: Some Books by David Bruce 73

Dedication

DEDICATED TO MY SISTER ROSA

The Doing of Good Deeds is Important

As a free person, you can choose to live your life as a good person or as a bad person. To be a good person, do good deeds. To be a bad person, do bad deeds. If you do good deeds, you will become good. If you do bad deeds, you will become bad. To become the person you want to be, act as if you already are that kind of person. Each of us chooses what kind of person we will become. To become a good person, do the things a good person does. To become a bad person, do the things a bad person does. The opportunity to take action to become the kind of person you want to be is yours.

"I Will Go with You Into the Grave"

In a medieval Christian mystery play, a man asks who will go with him into the grave when he dies and give him support at the Day of Judgment. Time after time, he hears the answer, "I won't go with you into the grave." His wife won't go with him into the grave, his children won't go with him into the grave, his priest won't go with him into the grave, his friends won't go with him into the grave — even his wealth won't go with him into the grave. Finally, the man's good deeds say, "I will go with you into the grave," and the man and his good deeds knock at the door of death, together. Your good deeds will plead for you on the Day of Judgment.

"Do Small Kindnesses for People"

Amy Alkon, aka "The Advice Goddess," does good deeds, and she used to write an advice column for alternative newspapers. She advises, "Do small kindnesses for people." For example, she buys and reads a newspaper every day. When she is finished reading it, she will look around wherever she is — often, she is in a café — and often see somebody who is looking for a newspaper. She will then ask, "Sir, would you like my newspaper?" She points out, "You've noticed a stranger, you've solved their problem, you've gone out of your way to do it, and they're gonna feel very good about that, and I think people will tend to pass on good deeds, do other good deeds, if you do good deeds for them." She adds that "it does make a difference."

"Dear"

One of the things that Kurt Vonnegut, Jr., believes firmly is this: "God d*mn it, you've got to be kind." One of the things that cheers him up is buying a morning cup of coffee in New York City, which he describes as mad for money. He says, "You can go into a little café and the waitress calls you 'dear' even though she knows the bill will be a small expenditure and the tip tiny. So she is responding to you as a person and feels happy and wants to communicate."

Show the Haters that They are Wrong

Robert DeMott and Dave Smith became friends in the early 1970s. They had a number of things in common that facilitated their friendship: they were or would become editors, scholars, teachers, and writers, plus both had been told as undergraduates by professors that they "were not smart enough or able enough to amount to much in the 'real' world" — predictions that they ignored. Mr. DeMott became a noted John Steinbeck scholar, and Mr. Smith became a noted poet.

"The Touchstone For What Good Deeds Became In My Life"

Donna Delfino Dugay of Harper Woods, Michigan, grew up in California, where her family had a picnic at the beach when she was 11 years old. Her mother fixed each of the children a plate of fried chicken and potato salad, and then, Donna says, "When I looked up from my plate, my mother was fixing one more plate .... She turned away from us and walked over maybe 20 or 30 feet to where there was a man by himself. And he was picking his way through the trashcan. And my mother — I don't know whether she just put the plate there or whether she touched him gently or whether she said a few words — but I remember him turning to her in a gesture of thankfulness." Years later, when Donna asked her mother about this good deed, her mother claimed not to remember it; however, Donna says, "But for me, I remember it very well because for me, it was the touchstone for what good deeds became in my life."

Cover Photograph for *The Funniest People in Television and Radio: 250 Anecdotes*:

Public Domain Cover Photograph: George Burns

https://en.wikipedia.org/wiki/George_Burns#/media/File:George_Burns_1961.JPG

Most of these anecdotes are funny; however, a few are thought provoking rather than funny.

All anecdotes have been retold in my own words to avoid plagiarism.

Chapter 1: From Actors to Autographs

Actors

• *Star Trek: The Experience* can be seen at the Las Vegas Hilton. Among other attractions are actors portraying characters from the various *Star Trek* series. Many of the actors are very good, and they stay in character. For example, a famous Ferengi is Quark. When a fan yelled "Quark!" at an actor in a Ferengi costume, the actor sighed and said, "Billions of Ferengi in the Universe, and they [Hu-Mans] all think we are Quark!" The Ferengi are a notoriously acquisitive species, and *Star Trek* fan Kevin Wagner was shocked that an actor playing a Ferengi agreed to pose for free for a photograph with a fan. Therefore, Kevin quoted the 13th Rule of Acquisition to the Ferengi: "Anything worth doing is worth doing for money." However, the actor playing the Ferengi knew his stuff: "Don't quote the Rules of Acquisition to me, Hu-Man. Free publicity!"[1]

• Fans of *Buffy the Vampire Slayer* were shocked in Season 2 when Angel, a bad vampire turned good, then bad again, killed the interesting and important character Jenny Calendar in the episode titled "Passion." According to an interview with series creator Josh Whedon, the killing of an interesting and important character served many purposes, including being a message to the actors: "Be very good or I'll kill you." (Mr. Whedon was joking. Robia LaMorte, the actress who played Jenny Calendar, was very, very good.)[2]

• Jack Riley played the character of the insulting, misanthropic Mr. Elliot Carlin on *The Bob Newhart Show*. One of his favorite episodes was "You're Fired, Mr. Chips," in which the great actor Ralph Bellamy co-starred. A consummate professional, Mr. Bellamy came to work the first day with all of his lines memorized. Mr. Riley asked Mr. Bellamy how he had learned his lines, and Mr. Bellamy replied, "The way I always did it. I keep the play in my back pocket. I'm standing in line at the supermarket, I got it out."[3]

• Panamanian actor Rubén Blades avoids jobs that involve his playing stereotypical Hispanic roles. Once, the people behind *Miami Vice* offered him the role of a Hispanic drug dealer. He turned them down. In one six-month period, he was offered 15 roles. Approximately half of the roles were Columbian drug dealers; the remaining roles were Cuban drug dealers. Mr. Blades, who has a degree in International Law from Harvard, asks, "Doesn't anybody want me to play a lawyer?"[4]

• In the days before women commonly became pregnant first, then got married, actress Paula Winslowe read a commercial over the radio that caused the studio audience to laugh. She read, "I am a June bride. My silverware pattern is International Silver's exquisite 'First Love.'" The audience began laughing after the first sentence because they could see that Ms. Winslowe's pregnancy was far too advanced for her to be a conventionally moral June bride.[5]

• Comedian Phil Foster (who played Laverne's father in *Laverne and Shirley*) and his wife knew an actress before she became famous, but when the actress got a TV series, she ignored the Fosters. But after the TV series was cancelled, she became friendly with them again. A few years later, the actress won a Supporting Actress Academy Award. Mr. Foster sent her this telegram: "CONGRATULATIONS — AND GOODBYE AGAIN."[6]

• Dick Gautier played Hymie the Robot in the 1960s TV series *Get Smart*. This was an unusual role, because Hymie spoke in a monotone and showed no emotion — the opposite of what an actor usually does. After Hymie had performed in a scene with Don Adams, who played Maxwell Smart, Mr. Adams would sometimes say, "Dick, that was absolutely one-dimensional," then give him a thumbs-up sign.[7]

• During the *Avengers* episode "Mandrake," Honor Blackman, who played Mrs. Cathy Gale, accidentally knocked out pro wrestler Jackie Pallo during a fight scene, kicking him in the face and knocking him backward into an open grave. He remained unconscious for six or seven minutes, and the newspapers had a field day with the story. For a while, Ms. Blackman was afraid that she had ruined his career.[8]

• Sarah Michelle Gellar, star of TV's *Buffy the Vampire Slayer*, in which she regularly killed vampires with a combination of karate moves and stakes to the heart, really got into the role. She once visited an amusement park where an actor dressed as a vampire jumped out to scare the amusement park visitors — Sarah gave the "vampire" a karate chop.[9]

• For a while, Ray Engle was the voice of old-time radio hero Sky King. He carried a gun and acted like a character out of the Old West. One day, when a director criticized his performance, Mr. Engle drew his gun, shouted, "You can't talk to Sky King like that!" — and shot a hole in a wall of the radio studio.[10]

• The hit TV series *Knight Rider*, featuring a car that had artificial intelligence and communicated using a human voice, started life as a joke. Brandon Tartikoff, an NBC executive, used to joke that he needed a TV series that starred a talking car so that the leading man wouldn't need much talent at acting.[11]

• Gypsy Rose Lee starred as Phyllis Diller's nosy neighbor in the TV sitcom *The Pruitts of Southampton*. Ms. Lee could be difficult. Getting ready to do the show one day, she started to scream. The man doing her hair complained, "I haven't even touched you." Ms. Lee replied, "But you're going to."[12]

• Alan Young got the part of Wilbur Post in *Mr. Ed* after George Burns, the show's producer (Mr. Burns became a TV producer after his wife, Gracie Allen, retired from show business), said, "I think we should get Alan Young. He looks like the kind of a guy that a horse would talk to."[13]

• In 1984, Lily Tomlin was nominated for an Emmy for an appearance as Ernestine the telephone operator in *Live ... and in Person*. Ms. Tomlin dressed as Ernestine at the awards ceremony — when she lost, Ernestine pouted.[14]

Ad-Libs

• While taping an appearance on TV in a special produced by Norman Lear called *I Love Liberty*, comedian Geri Jewell ran into a problem: No one was laughing. She stopped and told the audience, "I'm sorry. I need help. I need a line. I need ... someone to laugh." This ad-lib made the audience howl. Fortunately, Mr. Lear came on stage and told her what the problem had been — for the first part of her performance the microphone hadn't been working and so the audience couldn't hear her. She started over again, and this time the audience laughed throughout her performance.[15]

• In the days of live television, mistakes did happen. Ed Wynn once forgot his lines and couldn't see the cue cards. He ad-libbed, "I must have something to say — otherwise I wouldn't be standing here."[16]

Advertising

• In the 1960s, the advertising company W.B. Doner and Company created a series of TV commercials that asked about Tootsie Pops, "How many licks does it take to get to the Tootsie Roll center of a Tootsie Pop?" In one commercial, a young boy is advised by his angel side to keep on licking, while his devil side advises him to give in to temptation and bite the Tootsie Pop to get to the Tootsie Roll center quicker. The boy gives 187 licks before giving in to temptation and biting the Tootsie Pop. The commercial ends with these words: "How many licks does it take to get to the Tootsie Roll center of a Tootsie Pop? The world may never know." This commercial was so popular that people wrote the Tootsie Roll Company about how many licks it takes to get to the Tootsie Roll center of a Tootsie Pop. The company responded by giving the writers Clean Stick Award certificates.[17]

• In the early days of television, everything was live — which allowed for the opportunity to make mistakes. In Columbus, Ohio, a man named Spook Beckman often did a commercial for Big Bev hamburgers, in which he took a big bite out of a hamburger, then said (after pushing the food out of the way of his tongue), "Big Bev — it's delicious!" Unfortunately, the next thing the viewers saw one day was not the cartoon they were supposed to see. Due to a mistake at the TV studio, the viewers at home were treated to the sight of Mr. Beckman spitting the hamburger into a sink.[18]

• Balanchine ballerina Allegra Kent appeared in a few television commercials, some of which were very successful, but she did not get every part she auditioned for. In one case, a sadistic producer told her that she did not get the part because she was "not nubile enough." He also wanted her to recommend a nubile ballet dancer "aged 18 to 20." Ms. Kent responded, "Oh, gee, I just can't think of anybody that young, and you happen to be a tactless numbskull."[19]

• Henry Morgan was a comedian who knew how to treat a sponsor — like dirt. One of Mr. Morgan's radio sponsors (until they fired him) was the maker of the Oh Henry candy bars. While doing commercials for Oh Henry candy bars, Mr. Morgan would say, "Yes, Oh Henry is a meal in itself. But you eat three meals of Oh Henrys and your teeth will fall out." But Mr. Morgan did even worse than this — from the candy maker's viewpoint. After one commercial for Oh Henry candy bars, he told the radio audience, "Feed your children enough Oh Henrys, and they'll get sick and die."[20]

• Alka-Seltzer once had a very funny TV commercial in which a man making a commercial for spaghetti and meatballs keeps blowing his line — "*Mamma mia!* That's some spicy meatball!" — take after take, forcing him to consume more and more meatballs and causing indigestion, which is of course cured by Alka-Seltzer. In real life, the man making the commercial, Jack Somach, suffered through 175 takes, requiring him to bite into 175 meatballs. He skipped lunch and dinner that day.[21]

• Jack Benny's radio series occasionally made fun of its sponsors. For example, in one commercial, a telegram was read that supposedly came from a Canada Dry Ginger Ale salesman after he had found several people lost in the Sahara Desert without water for 40 days: "I came to their rescue, giving each of them a glass of Canada Dry. Not one of them said they didn't like it." (Believe it or not, Canada Dry stopped sponsoring *The Jack Benny* Show, and General Motors became the new sponsors.)[22]

• An actress was supposed to say these lines on a radio commercial: "Helen, darling, what a delightful necklace! It looks as if it had tiny real violets entwined in it. It speaks of springtime and the outdoors. It gives you an aura of freshness and youth, hope and beauty!" The actress performed flawlessly during rehearsals and during the performance, except that she forgot it was the performance and after saying her lines complained, "Do I actually have to say this garbage?"*[23]*

• When David Brenner appeared live on *The Ed Sullivan Show*, he was a major hit — the audience applauded so much that Mr. Sullivan brought him back on stage to take a bow. While acknowledging the audience's applause, however, Mr. Brenner looked at a TV monitor. The TV audience was seeing none of this wild audience enthusiasm, for after Mr. Brenner's final joke, the TV cameras had cut to a Preparation H commercial.[24]

• While appearing on *My Three Sons*, William Frawley (he also played Fred Mertz on *I Love Lucy*) and the other actors were required to do commercials for the sponsors' products. Mr. Frawley enjoyed the taping sessions when executives from Quaker Oats or Heinz were present. He used to take a bite of the sponsor's product, make a face, spit the food out, and then cuss while saying how bad it was.[25]

• In 1986, Michael Jackson made almost $15 million by appearing in two Pepsi TV commercials and serving as a consultant on a third commercial. The commercials did not show Mr. Jackson drinking Pepsi, and they did not show Mr. Jackson holding a Pepsi in his hand. Why not? Mr. Jackson is a Jehovah's Witness, and he does not drink beverages that contain caffeine — including Pepsi.[26]

• Jackie Gleason stood up for the integrity of *The Honeymooners*. His character, Ralph Kramden, lived in an apartment with an icebox

— the Kramdens were too poor to have a refrigerator. A refrigerator company offered to sponsor the show if the Kramdens got rid of the icebox and used one of its products, but Mr. Gleason refused.[27]

• In a very successful publicity stunt in 1933, Gracie's brother turned up missing, and Gracie wandered from radio show to radio show searching for him. In a tense radio drama featuring a submerged submarine, a character radioed the submarine captain and asked, "Is Gracie Allen's brother down there with you?"[28]

• Some celebrities are not for sale. Lily Tomlin once turned down $500,000 to have her character Ernestine ("One ringy-dingy. Two ringy-dingys. A gracious good morning to you. Have I reached the party to whom I am speaking?") perform in commercials for AT&T.[29]

Alcohol

• Dodgers president Branch Rickey used to talk to all the Dodgers once in a while, even the minor leaguers. One thing he stressed in his talks with the players was the importance of leading a good, morally pure life. One day, he talked to Chuck Connors, a minor-league Dodger first baseman. He asked Chuck, "Son, do you smoke?" Chuck answered, "No, sir, Mr. Rickey." He then asked, "Chuck, do you run around with fast women?" Chuck answered, "No, sir." Next, Mr. Rickey asked, "Do you drink hard liquor?" This time Chuck answered, "Mr. Rickey, if I have to drink to play for you, I want to be traded." (And yes, this is the Chuck Connors who later starred in the TV series *The Rifleman*.)[30]

• When brothers Glen and Les Charles and friend James Burrows set about creating *Cheers*, they did research in bars. They discovered that often people go to bars for the companionship, not for the alcohol, and that is the kind of bar they chose for *Cheers* to be set in. At one bar, they heard the regulars discussing soup. Les Charles remembers, "We were sitting there, listening to them have this extended conversation about soup. They were all really into it. ... They were having the time of their lives." For an episode of *Cheers*, they had the regulars discuss the world's sweatiest movie — another topic of conversation they had heard discussed in a friendly neighborhood bar.[31]

• At a BBC Light Entertainment Christmas party, Monty Python member Graham Chapman started crawling around the floor biting people's ankles. This joke started to get out of hand, so Monty Python TV director Ian MacNaughton went over to him and said, "Graham, can you just select whose ankles you bite?" Mr. Chapman stood up, brushed himself off, said, "I get the picture, old boy," and behaved like a gentleman during the rest of the party.[32]

• *Cavalcade of America* once devoted an entire broadcast to Alcoholics Anonymous, but ran into a problem with the name of the announcer: Tom Collins. He was able to help disguise the problem by using a middle initial when he stated his name at the sign-off.[33]

• The then-President of CBS, Bill Paley, once came into the dressing room of George Burns and Gracie Allen with a bottle of champagne. He poured glassfuls all around, then said, "Bottoms up." Gracie asked, "Isn't that an awkward position for drinking?"[34]

• Ernie Kovacs used to own a watch on which every hour — instead of being 1 through 12 — was 5. In other words, no matter what time it was, it was the cocktail hour.[35]

Animals

• Early in her career, actress Betty White lived in an apartment where pets weren't allowed. However, she fell in love with a dog and brought him home. To get her dog past the security guards so he could take his morning walk, she used to hold him on her arm and throw a coat over him. For a long time, she thought she was fooling everyone, until one day a security guard said to her, "Miss White, your tail is wagging." She looked down, and sure enough, her dog's tail was sticking out from under the coat and wagging. The security guard grinned and allowed her to keep her pet. (Betty White came from a family who loved pets. In her family, it was the parents who brought a dog home, then begged, "Betty, he followed us home. Please, can we keep him?")[36]

• Vincent Price once appeared in a comic skit on TV in which his co-star was a trained chimpanzee that was supposed to mix a martini and then light a cigarette. The chimp mixed the martini without any problem, but ignored the cigarettes in take after take. Finally, the chimpanzee's trainer figured out what the problem was — the cigarettes used in the filming weren't the chimp's brand! Once the chimp's preferred brand of mentholated cigarettes were used in the scene, the chimp lit the cigarette.[37]

• Many people enjoyed listening to Milton Cross as he announced the radio broadcasts of the Metropolitan Opera — so did some animals. A letter to the Met reported, "I'm not particularly fond of Milton Cross' voice, but my dog loves it. As soon as I turn on the radio and Cross comes over the airwaves, the pooch remains glued to the set. When the music starts, he leaves. As soon as Cross is on again, the dog is back — all ears."[38]

• Columbus, Ohio, radio deejay Bob Simpson once asked listeners for silly pet names. One caller had a friend who had named his cat "Stir Fry." Why? "It's a threat." By the way, Channel 4 (Columbus, Ohio) News once gave a quiz to help determine if you are a hypochondriac. After giving the quiz, the news co-anchor, Colleen Marshall, said, "If you think you are a hypochondriac, you should see a doctor."[39]

• When Patrick Macnee shared an apartment with fellow actor Dennis Price, he ran into a problem. Mr. Price kept a flock of chickens in the bathroom. One advantage was that the roommates always had fresh eggs for breakfast, although there were also some obvious disadvantages. When Mr. Macnee remonstrated with Mr. Price about the chickens, Mr. Price asked, "Can you lay eggs?"[40]

• Comedian Wally Cox (TV's Mr. Peepers) was a bird expert. At his farm in Connecticut, birds even flew to him and rested on his hands and arms. One of his friends wanted very much to do this. She learned the proper birdcalls, but the birds wouldn't come to her the way they came to Wally. Finally, the woman put on Wally's hat and coat — seconds later, she was covered with birds.[41]

• During World War II, Spike Milligan and some fellow soldiers were shipped to Algiers. On the voyage, the soldiers became trigger-happy, frequently firing anti-aircraft guns at seagulls. Eventually, the ship's Captain told them, "Gentlemen, all seagulls in this area are unarmed. Can we refrain from shooting at them?"[42]

• Ballet dancer Rudolf Nureyev once watched a nature show during which a sheep carcass was thrown into the Everglades, where frenzied alligators immediately devoured it. Mr. Nureyev recognized the scene: "Ah, Paris Opéra."[43]

• Jack Webb, star of *Dragnet*, took steps not to be overwhelmed by success. To remind himself to be humble, he kept a photograph of his Hollywood Walk of Fame star — on which a dog had left a stinky memento.[44]

Auditions

• In the early days of television, when most shows were live, many local stations featured homegrown talent, which meant that TV directors such as Paul Ritts were "treated" to a variety show weekly as they tried to find a few people with actual talent to put on the air. Of course, actual talent was frequently absent (many of the TV people working during the auditions turned off their earphones until after the auditions were over), although some performers tried to make up for it with deviousness. Often, these performers would find an excuse to speak to the person auditioning talent after the audition was over; that way, they could make a plug for themselves. One day, a pretty dancer who was much more talented at being pretty than she was at dancing stopped by Mr. Ritts' office to explain that she had "mistakenly" written her old address instead of her new address on a form she had filled out. Mr. Ritts got the form out so he could make the correction, and the pretty dancer sat down and crossed her legs. Since she was still wearing her dance costume — which was both scanty and flimsy and only sort of covered by a scanty and flimsy outer garment, the crossing of her legs was an event of interest to almost any man and more than a few women. One of those women happened to be Mr. Ritts' wife, who walked into his office, looked at the dancer's legs, remarked that dresses were definitely getting shorter, and then paid a visit to her husband's boss. Shortly afterward, Mr. Ritts received a note from his boss informing him that due to his many other duties someone else would henceforward audition talent.[45]

• Pop star and actress Brandy attended the Hollywood High Performing Arts Center, where she studied acting and singing. She thought that her drama teacher would recommend her for auditions, but that didn't happen. One day, Brandy asked her drama teacher, "Why aren't you sending me out on calls?" The teacher replied, "Because you're not drop-dead gorgeous." The criticism didn't stop Brandy, who starred as Cinderella on television. By the way, one person who had faith in Brandy's talents from the beginning was Brandy's mother, who, after giving birth to Brandy, told her physician, "You just birthed a star."[46]

• David Hasselhoff starred in *Baywatch*, which was a huge international hit. Earlier, he had struggled as an actor, and so he was kind to struggling actors. Often, after a first scene in an audition he knew that he could not use a particular actor in the TV series, but he would allow the actor to do a second scene anyway. Why? He says he did this "because I knew they'd practiced, because I knew how much it hurt me when I got rejected when I first started."[47]

• Early in her career, Lucille Ball wanted to be a showgirl. During one audition, producers lined the women up in a line, then walked down the line, looking the women over. Lucy knew that some of the other women were better endowed than she, so she stuffed her bodice with toilet paper. Unfortunately, some of the toilet paper was sticking out of her bodice — this did get Lucy noticed![48]

Autographs

• Diana Rigg, who played the very sexy Mrs. Emma Peel on *The Avengers*, once declined to sign an autograph for a fan by saying, "I'm sorry, but it's illegal to sign autographs in the street." (It's not, of course.) It was Ms. Rigg's mother who answered fan mail from overeager youths by writing, "My daughter is much too old for you and what you need is a good run around the block."[49]

• A woman was a little too much obsessed with soap opera *Another World* star Paul Michael Valley. Once Mr. Valley fell and hit his head on a fireplace mantle on the set. He was put on a stretcher to be rushed to the hospital when a woman handed him a pen and asked for his autograph, saying, "I know this is a bad time ...."[50]

Chapter 2: From Bathrooms to Education

Bathrooms

• An English lady — Miss Jean Marsh, actress (star of *Upstairs, Downstairs*) — was given a crash course in American euphemisms before coming to New York City for the first time. Her mentors told her that in American polite society, one does not use the word "toilet." Instead, one uses such phrases and words as "ladies room," "powder room," "restroom," and "lounge." She arrived at a television studio in New York City, where a man was to give her a tour. But first he asked her, "Before I take you on a tour of the studio, would you like to use the facilities?" Miss Marsh replied, "Oh, no, I'm not mechanical at all — I'd be afraid to touch anything!"[51]

• When Robert L. Mott was working for the *Captain Kangaroo Show* live on TV, his sound effects room was located next to the building's only women's restroom. The flushes from this bathroom were very loud, and Mr. Mott understandably did not want the sound of the flushes to be heard on the children's program; therefore, before each show started, he put an "Out of Order" sign on the door of the restroom. One show, he had just turned on the microphone for a sound effect on the show, when a woman screeched, "OUT OF ORDER! OH, F**K!"[52]

• When Tracey Ullman was 13 years old, she heard a knock on the door. When she answered it, she discovered a woman, who asked to use the bathroom. Tracey led the woman to the bathroom, which turned out to be a mistake because the woman was a bag lady who locked the door, then proceeded to take a shower, wash her hair, and shave her legs. Finally, Tracey's stepfather picked the lock and was able to get her out of their home.[53]

• In the 1960s, Ethel Winant was the head of casting for CBS, and as head of casting, she was a powerful woman at a time when few powerful women existed in television. In fact, no women's restroom was close to her office. Whenever she needed to make use of a restroom, she went to the men's restroom — and left her high heels outside the door so her male co-workers would know not to enter.[54]

Cartoons

• Bill Hanna and Joe Barbera worked together on many *Tom and Jerry* cartoons, as well as cartoons starring the characters The Flintstones, The Jetsons, Huckleberry Hound, Yogi Bear, and Scoobie-Doo. Both were capable of causing mischief. When they were youngsters, Bill and Norma, his sister, cracked every window in the family's barn. Of course, they had a good reason: They liked the patterns the cracked windows made. As a cartoonist working on *Tom and Jerry*, Joe once drilled a hole in a wall, then he inserted a soda straw into the hole. When the cartoonist who worked in the office next door sat down, Joe filled his mouth with water, then used the straw to spray the back of the cartoonist's head with water. This is the artistic sensibility and the sense of humor that resulted in the *Tom and Jerry* cartoons winning seven Academy Awards. Nowadays, of course, the *Tom and Jerry* cartoons are shown on television.[55]

• Leon Schlesinger was cartoon director Tex Avery's boss, and he was a very hard man to get money from. However, he loved to gamble, so when Mr. Avery wanted a $25 raise, Mr. Schlesinger proposed that they draw cards to see who got the highest-value playing card. If Mr. Schlesinger won, Mr. Avery would get no raise. If Mr. Avery won, then he would get a $50 raise. Fortunately for Mr. Avery, he won — jack to eight.[56]

Censorship

• Tommy Smothers realized that his 1960s TV variety show *The Smothers Brothers Comedy Hour* was controversial, and he knew that it was only a matter of time before the censors would start making very strong "requests" to tone down the satire — especially the political satire. He had a decision to make: either fight to keep the satire or be bought off and lose the satire. He could fight the censors, or he could continue to live the easy life of a major television celebrity with lots of money, lots of cars, and lots of houses. He made his decision. He sold off cars and houses to reduce the kind of expenses that make courage difficult, fought the censors, and eventually his show was cancelled despite its coveted high ratings among younger people with lots of disposable income. Of course, by that time Mr. Smothers had made being fired affordable.[57]

• In the early days of radio, producers avoided controversy; however, feminist Olga Petrova got her point across anyway. Before Ms. Petrova's program of singing, the station manager asked what she planned to say on the air. She replied, "Just a few nursery stories like 'The Old Woman Who Lived in a Shoe.'" There's nothing controversial about nursery stories, is there? Wrong. On the air, Ms. Petrova said, "There was an old woman who lived in a shoe. She had so many children because she didn't know what to do." Before the station manager realized the satiric meaning of what she had said, it had already been broadcast.[58]

Children

• Tori Spelling's father was Aaron Spelling, a spectacularly successful and wealthy TV magnate. Because of her family connection, Tori co-starred in *Beverly Hills, 90210*. Growing up in such a wealthy family led to experiences that were much different from those of lower- and middle-class kids, although for Tori they were the only experiences she knew. For example, she got a nose job as a teenager, and her mother reserved one room out of a 123-room mansion for the sole purpose of wrapping presents. In addition, when Tori was very young, her father trucked in several tons of snow so that she could enjoy a white Christmas in Los Angeles.[59]

• Lucille Ball was born in Celoron (a suburb of Jamestown), New York, on August 6, 1911. When she was almost four, her father died, and the family was taken under the wing of her mother's father, "Grandpa" Fred Hunt. A few months after her father's death, Lucy wore a harness that was tied to a trolley on a clothesline so she could run around in the yard but couldn't run next door to visit some kids who had measles. Her mother overheard Lucy talking to the milkman: "Oh, mister, somehow I happened to get caught in this silly old clothesline. Do you think you could get me loose?"[60]

• In the early days of television, TV sets were dangerous — it took 42,000 volts of electricity to operate them. When Wayne Halverson, a childhood friend of author Gary Paulsen, turned 12, he licked the end of his finger then brought it close to the ventilation panel of his family's TV. An arc of electricity grabbed him, threw him against a wall, and knocked him unconscious for several minutes. Later, Wayne discovered that the incident had given him a superpower similar to those of comic-book characters — Wayne was the first in his group of young male buddies to be able to talk to girls.[61]

• Art Linkletter became famous in large part because of his interviews of children on his various TV programs. He would chat with the children a few minutes before they went on the air in order to find out who would be a good interview subject. Occasionally, a child would be so hyperactive that Mr. Linkletter would be forced to calm the child down by being "stern" with the child — for example, Mr. Linkletter would sometimes tell a hyperactive child to be on his best behavior because the President of the United States would be watching the show.[62]

• R.L. Stine worked as a writer on the TV series *Eureeka's Castle*, which featured many puppets, including a large puppet of a dragon that took as many as three people to operate. The people behind the TV series received a letter from the mother of a young girl who wanted to visit the set, and they invited the mother and the young girl to visit. Unfortunately, when the young girl arrived, she looked around the set and then started crying — she was disappointed because she had thought that the characters of *Eureeka's Castle* were real.[63]

• As young children with cerebral palsy, which affected their muscle control, comedian Geri Jewell and her best friend, Christine Kellogg, enjoyed watching the children's TV show *Engineer Bill.* Among other educational games, Engineer Bill taught children to drink all their milk by use of a game called "Red Light, Green Light." When he said "Green Light," the children were supposed to drink their milk, but when he said "Red Light," the children were supposed to stop. Because of their cerebral palsy, Geri and Christine spilled more milk than they drank.[64]

• Madeleine L'Engle, author of *A Wrinkle in Time*, and her husband, Hugh Franklin, a professional actor who played Dr. Charles Tyler on the TV soap opera *All My Children*, decided to move back to New York City after years of living in the country. They explained to their three children that cities were much different from the country, and that they could take only one of their seven cats and only one of their three dogs with them. Their youngest child opened his eyes wide and asked, "And only one child?"[65]

• When she was a little girl, comedian Carol Burnett pretended that she had an identical twin sister named Karen, and she tried to convince the neighbors that Karen really existed. Therefore, Carol would go home to her apartment, change clothes quickly, leave using the fire escape, then reappear in the front door of the apartment house as Karen. Eventually, Carol grew exhausted trying to be two people, so Karen left on an extended vacation from which she never returned.[66]

• Tex Avery created the personality of Bugs Bunny and directed many cartoons starring the character, as well as some Kool-Aid TV commercials featuring Bugs. When some little kids found out that he had some cels and drawings of Bugs Bunny in his car, he gave them to the kids. Soon after, a little girl asked him for more. He replied, "I gave you a whole batch of them!" She said, "But my brother takes them to school and sells them for fifty cents apiece!"[67]

• TV's Mister Rogers once attended a children's program at an outreach facility. Because he did not want his celebrity to detract from the attention that ought to be given to the children, he and his wife sneaked into the auditorium. However, the children knew that he would be attending, and they wanted to see where he was sitting, so during the program, one of the children yelled, "Where you at, Mister Rogers? Where you at?"[68]

• *Gilligan's Island* is very popular with children. Bob Denver, who played Gilligan, tells this story: One small child ran inside after playing in her backyard every afternoon just in time to watch the show. Her mother asked how she knew *Gilligan's Island* was on — after all, the little girl didn't know how to tell time yet. She replied that when the sun touched the top of the big tree, it was time to watch "Giggle'ns Island."[69]

• Eve Arden, star of *Our Miss Brooks*, once had a problem because Liza, her older — but still very young — daughter, kept hitting Connie, Ms. Arden's even younger daughter. Hoping that Liza would transfer her anger in another direction, Ms. Arden bought a Bozo the Clown punching doll for her to hit. Unfortunately, the plan didn't work. Liza complained, "I don't want to hit poor Bozo. I'm not mad at him. I'm mad at Connie."[70]

• When actor Patrick Macnee, star of *The Avengers*, went away to a boarding school, he and the other small boys were leery of changing their clothes where others could see them, and so they changed under sheets and behind curtains. One boy even climbed out the window and slid down a drainpipe, changed clothes outdoors, then climbed back up the drainpipe and in through the window.[71]

• Nancy Cartwright's children grew up knowing that their mother supplied the voice of TV's Bart Simpson, and sometimes they let other kids in on this fact. One day, Ms. Cartwright found herself surrounded by a bunch of Cub Scouts, who begged her, “Do Bart! Do Bart!” She obliged, and then she heard her son say, “See, I told you my mom was Bart Simpson!”[72]

• Lloyd Bridges was a rugged action hero in movies for many years. One day Sandy, his young daughter, appeared on Art Linkletter’s *House Party*. Mr. Linkletter, who is famous in large part because of his interviews with children, asked Sandy, “Who’s the real boss in your family?” She answered, “Daddy’s the boss in the movies. Mom’s the boss at home.”[73]

• An early home movie of TV’s Mister Rogers shows him as a toddler. His father keeps putting a hat on his head, and the young Mister Rogers keeps grabbing the hat. Mister Rogers uses this anecdote to illustrate what a Dr. McFarland calls “hungry hands.” Toddlers have a need to touch things and explore them with their hands.[74]

• Even in the 4th grade, Jay Leno was funny. During class, his teacher showed slides of an Egyptian mummy. On the slide of the mummy appeared the caption, “2050 BCE.” When the teacher asked if anyone knew what the caption meant, Jay replied, “That’s the license number of the truck that hit him.”[75]

• Judy Pioli Ervin, a producer of the TV sitcom *Laverne and Shirley*, used to perform when she was a child for her parents’ friends. She would sit at an organ and play Lawrence Welk music, while her younger sister sat hidden behind the organ and blew bubbles. She always got the laughs she wanted.[76]

• As a child, TV’s Mister Rogers occasionally became angry, but he wasn’t allowed to stomp around the house to work out his anger. However, he was allowed to play his emotions on the piano. He usually began by banging out single notes, but after a while, he started to play calm music.[77]

• As a child, Carol Burnett used to pretend to be an entire radio show. She would open her window wide, then shout out all the parts of the pretend show — announcer, guest singer, etc. One day, she felt complimented when a neighbor shouted, "Turn that d*mn radio off!"[78]

Clothing

• Bill D'Arcy, the first assistant director on *Gilligan's Island*, got a big break when he was asked to direct an episode of the TV sitcom. He had been very easy going as an assistant director, but on his first day of work as a director, he showed up dressed as an autocratic Austrian-German director (think of Erich von Stroheim, Fritz Lang, and Otto Preminger) with beret, riding crop, monocle, riding breeches, knee-high boots — the works. With an Austrian-German accent, he announced that the set would have no fooling around while he was the director. Then he set up everything for the first scene. Everything was ready and the actors waited for him to say "Action!" Unfortunately, his nerves got the better of him, and he yelled "Cut!" instead. After that mistake, and a lot of teasing from the crew and cast, Mr. D'Arcy of course jettisoned the joke of the autocratic Austrian-German director, and he became a fine director.[79]

• Geraldo Rivera once interviewed Holly Woodlawn, who was born male but who looked fabulous in women's clothing. Mr. Rivera kept asking Ms. Woodlawn nosy questions, and he even wanted to look under her skirt, but she skillfully deflected his questions and declined to let him look under her skirt. Finally, Mr. Rivera demanded, "Please answer me. What are you? Are you a woman trapped in a man's body? Are you a heterosexual? Are you a homosexual? A transvestite? A transsexual? What is the answer to the question?" Ms. Woodlawn replied, "But, darling, what difference does it make as long as you look fabulous?"[80]

• Honor Blackman wore a lot of leather outfits when she played Mrs. Cathy Gale on the British tongue-in-cheek TV series *The Avengers*. Her role required a lot of physical activity, as Mrs. Gale never screamed for help when attacked, but instead responded with judo. After splitting her pants in a scene, she knew that she needed stronger costumes to perform in. Patrick Macnee, who played John Steed in the series, suggested leather, and a new fashion statement was born.[81]

• Eve Arden was the star of *Our Miss Brooks*, featuring a sometimes sarcastic but always loveable schoolteacher. After being criticized for the wardrobe she wore on the TV series — her clothing was way too expensive for a schoolteacher — Ms. Arden started shopping for costumes that a schoolteacher could afford to wear.[82]

• George Lindsey played Goober for a few years on *The Andy Griffith Show* — a role that has stayed with him. One day, he was walking in the Knoxville, Tennessee, airport while wearing sunglasses, a trench coat, and a mustache — but a boy still spotted him and yelled, "Mama, there's Goober with a mustache!"[83]

• Reggie Smith was both the prop man on *The Andy Griffith Show* and a member of a nudist colony. Don Knotts, who played Deputy Barney Fife, once got a laugh by saying on a Friday afternoon, "Everybody's going away for the weekend, and Reggie's the only one who doesn't have to pack."[84]

Comedians

• Carl Reiner, creator of *The Dick Van Dyke Show*, decided that he wanted to do something different from the first year's opening montage of photographs of the cast, so he decided to use Mr. Van Dyke's gift for physical comedy and keep the audience guessing. Therefore, he had two opening segments for the show filmed. The first shows Mr. Van Dyke tripping over an ottoman in the sitcom living room, while the second shows him deftly sidestepping the ottoman. These opening segments were used randomly on the episodes. A third segment was filmed later; it showed Mr. Van Dyke deftly sidestepping the ottoman, then stumbling.[85]

• Joan Rivers was thin, and she didn't mind making fun of fat celebrities. Back when Elizabeth Taylor had gained weight, she became one of Ms. Rivers' favorite comedic targets: "Elizabeth Taylor is so fat, when she pierces her ears gravy comes out." (Ms. Taylor was a good sport about it.) Roseanne, on the other hand, is fat, and she doesn't like it when thin people make fun of fat people. She says, "What I would say to Joan is, 'Yeah, I eat just like you. I just don't puke when I'm through.'" About herself, Roseanne says, "You're looking at one happy fat b*tch."[86]

• Durward Kirby was the announcer on *The Garry Moore Show*, and he was also a comedian in many of the show's sketches. Colleagues remember one sketch in which a comic gangster shot his character many, many times with a machine gun, and the character took a long time to fall to the floor and "die." Later, Mr. Kirby explained that the stage floor had been dirty, and he had simply been looking for a clean spot to die on.[87]

• Fred Allen was amazingly funny on radio, but he was never a hit on TV, which he disliked. A hotel manager once gave Bob Hope a basket of fruit, which Mr. Hope put on top of the TV in his hotel room. Fred Allen walked into the hotel room, saw the basket of fruit, smiled, and then told Mr. Hope, "You know, that's the best thing I've seen on television yet."[88]

• Arsenio Hall suffered from an attack of the nerves before his first attempt at stand-up comedy. When he heard his name called to go to the stage, he didn't run up to the stage — he ran out the door.[89]

Critics

• TV critic Anne Billson wrote a critical analysis of *Buffy the Vampire Slayer*, an American cult TV series that she greatly admired because of its strong female, action-oriented role model. Despite her great love of the series, she did not like some characters. One was Dawn, Buffy's younger sister (sort of) in seasons 5-7, whom Ms. Billman (and many *Buffy* fans) criticizes for being whiny. At the end of season 5, Buffy saves Dawn (and the world) by sacrificing her life. While watching the episode, Ms. Billman found herself screaming at the TV screen, "FOR GOD'S SAKE, LET THEM TAKE DAWN INSTEAD!" Ms. Billman's extreme dislike of Dawn continued throughout seasons 6 and 7 of *Buffy*. When Ms. Billman lists a number of actions performed by Evil Willow at the end of season 6, one item (with Ms. Billman's commentary) is this: "terrorize Dawn (yay!)." In the final episode of the final season of *Buffy* (season 7), Ms. Billman knew that an important character would be killed. In her book about the show, she writes, "But who will be sacrificed? Xander or Willow? Giles? Faith? Principal Wood? Or (please, please) Dawn?" To be fair, Michelle Trachtenberg, who played Dawn, also thought that the character was whiny. She once pleaded with Joss Whedon, the creator of *Buffy*, to let the character be less whiny — and wear high heels (or at least pumps). After the series ended, a *Rocky Horror*-type audience-participation showing of the musical episode of *Buffy* — "Once More, With Feeling" — began happening in some major American cities. Whenever Dawn is whiny in the episode, the audience yells, "SHUT UP, DAWN!"[90]

• Fred Allen was contemptuous of authority in general and his sponsors (who censored his scripts) in particular. One day, while Mr. Allen was warming up the audience for his radio show, a light was turned on in the booth where the sponsor of the show usually sat, but the light revealed that no one was in the booth. "Ladies and gentleman," Mr. Allen told the audience, "that booth is a device to belittle the comedian by showing him that the sponsor doesn't care enough for his program to attend it." A pageboy went to the booth and turned off the light. Mr. Allen then announced, "Ah, a boy who has the guts to turn off a light without a memo from a vice-president will go right to the top of the organization."[91]

• Jerry Mander wrote a book in 1978 titled *Four Arguments for the Elimination of Television*. Of course, immediately many TV programs wanted to book Mr. Mander as a guest — which Mr. Mander refused to do. Once a TV producer called him and asked him to sum up his book in a few words. Mr. Mander replied that he could not do that; after all, it had taken him 100,000 words to write his book. The producer then asked Mr. Mander what were his main points. Mr. Mander replied, "One of the main points is that television can only deal with main points."[92]

• Humorist Frank Sullivan had a sister named Kate, who bought a TV in the days when TVs were rare. Very quickly, she called a TV repairman, who asked, "What seems to be wrong with it?" She replied, "Well, for one thing, a lot of the programs are lousy."[93]

Death

• At the end of season 5 of *Buffy the Vampire Slayer*, Buffy dies, shocking the fans of the series. Actually, not just the fans were shocked. James Marsters, who played the role of Spike the vampire, pleaded with series creator Joss Whedon not to kill Buffy. He argued, "Joss, you can't kill Buffy. The show is called *Buffy the Vampire Slayer*! You can't do that, man — I need the job!" Mr. Whedon looked Mr. Marsters in the eyes and said, "Dude, it's my show. I can do whatever I want." (By the way, Mr. Whedon really can do whatever he wants — he brought Buffy back to life the following season. Actually, he had done that before — this was the second time that Buffy had died.)[94]

• Pat Leno, Jay's brother, served in Vietnam. Of course, any family with a member serving in Vietnam dreaded receiving telegrams because that was the means the Pentagon used to announce that a soldier or sailor had died. One day, the Leno family received a telegram. They looked at the telegram for 10 minutes, afraid to open it and see what it said. Finally, Jay's father opened it and read, "YOU ARE INVITED TO WENTWORTH CHEVROLET TO VIEW THE EXCITING NEW CAPRICE CLASSIC!" Jay's father bought many cars during the rest of his life — none of them was a Chevy.[95]

• Late in life, Fanny Brice — radio's Baby Snooks — enjoyed interior decorating, often decorating her friends' houses for free (and disregarding their advice while doing so). She acquired her good taste in decorating through asking questions constantly and not pretending like she already knew everything. She also began talking about where to leave her money after she died. One day, when one of her little grandchildren was making more racket than usual, she said, "One more crack out of you, kid, and the money goes to UCLA."[96]

• Blossom Rock provided comic support in 1940s movies (and played Grandmama on TV's *Addams Family*). In 1938, she and her husband hosted a party in which everybody came as they thought they would be in 50 years. Ms. Rock wore a tombstone. (Her costume was accurate; she died in 1978.)[97]

Education

• In high school, Pam Dawber liked to talk to her friends, even during choir. However, her teacher, Mr. Hunt, had a policy of giving students an F for the day if he caught them talking. During Pam's senior year, Mr. Hunt told her that her talking in class had dropped her grade in choir to a D, but he would give her a C if she tried out for a singing role in the high school production of the musical *Kismet*. She did try out, she got the role, she discovered that she liked acting, and she decided to make it her life's work. Today, she is widely known for playing "Mindy" in *Mork and Mindy*.[98]

• As Michael Moore, director of *Roger and Me*, was watching Sunday morning television, he came across a political commentary program on which Fred Barnes, a conservative, deplored the state of modern American education, saying, "These kids don't even know what *The Iliad* and *The Odyssey* are!" The next day, Mr. Moore telephoned Mr. Barnes, and he asked, "Fred, tell me what *The Iliad* and *The Odyssey* are." Mr. Barnes replied, "Well, they're ... uh ... you know ... uh ... okay, fine, you got me — I don't know what they're about. Happy now?"[99]

• Russell Johnson, who played the Professor on *Gilligan's Island*, could have been a good teacher. In Philadelphia, an educational channel conducted an experiment. First, it showed a class such clips as the Professor explaining how he recharged batteries from different metals and seawater, and how he made glass from sand, etc. Then a different class was taught the same information by a professional teacher. Evaluation of the two classes showed that the class watching the Professor learned the information four times as well as the other class.[100]

• James Marsters, who played the vampire Spike on TV's *Buffy the Vampire Slayer*, knew that he wanted to be an actor after playing Eeyore the mournful donkey in a 4th-grade play. Unfortunately, after deciding what he wanted to do with his life, he was no longer interested in anything in school except what was relevant to acting. His mother made a valiant effort to convince him that chemistry and higher math were relevant to acting — but her effort was mainly unsuccessful.[101]

• When Oprah Winfrey was five years old and in kindergarten, she wrote a letter to her teacher, saying that she felt that she deserved to be in a higher grade. Her teacher agreed, perhaps because Oprah had started to learn to read when she was only two and a half years old, and put Oprah in the 1st grade. Later, because of her educational attainments, Oprah was able to skip the 2nd grade, too.[102]

Chapter 3: From Fame to Language

Fame

• When comedian Alan Young got his own radio show, his agent told him that he would now be famous and lots of people would be very willing to take up his time. His agent also told him, "You are an important man now. Don't waste your time talking to just anybody." Later that day, an elderly gentleman started talking to him, but Mr. Young told him that he was busy. Then he whispered to his agent and asked who the elderly gentleman was. His agent whispered back, "That's Lee Bristol, your sponsor."[103]

• David Hasselhoff starred in the TV series *Knight Rider*, in which his character played a good guy who drove around in a car named Kitt that had lots of artificial intelligence. *Knight Rider* was internationally popular, and when Mr. Hasselhoff was driving in Auckland, New Zealand, he saw two schoolchildren carrying *Knight Rider* backpacks. When he came near them, he stopped the car, rolled down the window, and asked, "Have you seen Kitt?"[104]

• Comedian Gracie Allen became so famous that whenever she went out in public, autograph seekers surrounded her. At the height of her celebrity, Gracie was accompanied in public by a person who watched the crowd of people surrounding her. Whenever the crowd became too large, the person would loudly say, "I'm sorry, Miss Allen, but you have to leave right now. They're waiting for you at the studio."[105]

Fans

• USAmericans sometimes have a wonderful sense of humor. For example, many of us older men wonder what it would be like to be Cary Grant for a few days. (For you younger people, Cary Grant was the Brad Pitt of his day.) Comic songwriter Allan Sherman (writer of "Hello Mudduh, Hello Fadduh"), a short, stocky man, actually got the chance to be Cary Grant. As the guest host of *The Tonight Show* (back when Johnny Carson was king of late nights), Mr. Sherman told the television audience at the beginning of his week as guest host that he wanted to be Cary Grant for a week. During the next few days, hundreds of people asked Mr. Sherman for Cary Grant's autograph, which Mr. Sherman signed for them. In addition, the post office delivered to Mr. Sherman thousands of letters addressed to "Cary Grant, New York City," and a model stopped Mr. Sherman on the street and told him, "You look much younger in person, Mr. Grant."[106]

• Of course, TV stars run into problems that non-celebrities don't. One problem is that the viewers of TV programs tend to think that they know a character on TV rather than understanding that they are watching an actor portraying a character. Michael Urie plays a gay character on TV's *Ugly Betty*, and many, many people like the character. While he and his family were vacationing in Yosemite, he heard a woman yell, "Ahh! I love you! I love you!" — then she came over and hugged him. Mr. Urie says, "It's pretty awkward sometimes. It's like oh, my god, I don't know you, but they come up to you with this look. For the first several months when that would happen, I just assumed I did know them, because they seemed to know me so well. I've gotten a little more accustomed to it."[107]

• Lionel Barrymore was a big fan of the 1950s children's TV show *Time for Beany*, featuring "Uncle Captain" Huffenpuff and Cecil the Seasick Sea Serpent. One day, he was hurrying home to try to make it in time to see *Time for Beany*. When he knew that he wouldn't make it in time, he had his chauffeur pull over at a house with a TV antenna, then ask the family if he, the chauffeur, could watch *Time for Beany*. (Mr. Barrymore would have watched it, but he was in a wheelchair in those days.) After the show was over, Mr. Barrymore made his chauffeur tell him — in detail — what had happened on the show.[108]

• TV critic Anne Billson longed for strong female, action-oriented role models when she was growing up. Fortunately, she found one in Emma Peel, John Steed's equal in the British cult TV series *The Avengers*. Emma Peel was played by Diana Rigg, whom 30 years later

Ms. Billson met in a line for the women's lavatories. Like so many fans do, Ms. Billson blurted out, "You were my role model!" Ms. Rigg graciously replied, "Why, thank you," then Ms. Billson added, "And you still are."[109]

• Filmmaker John Waters was a huge fan of an old TV program titled *Lie Detector*, which starred F. Lee Bailey and which featured criminals claiming to be innocent and taking lie detector tests. One of Mr. Waters' friends was chosen to tell the Nielsen ratings people what shows he watched. Since Mr. Waters liked the program so much, he paid his friend to lie and record in his Nielsen diary that he watched the program. Unfortunately, this attempt to boost the program's ratings failed and *Lie Detector* was cancelled.[110]

• Many gay men love *The Mary Tyler Moore Show*, whose lead character, Mary Richards, had a big "M" hanging on the wall of her apartment. (When the series was over, everyone associated with the show took an item from Ms. Richards' apartment as a memento; Ms. Moore took the M.) In fact, one gay interior decorator insists on hanging a big "M" on a wall of each home he decorates.[111]

• Often, fans want to make friends with celebrities. Before starring in his sitcom, stand-up comedian Jerry Seinfeld was at a car wash when a man who had seen his act came up to him and asked, "Could we be friends?" Mr. Seinfeld replied, "Well, that's really the nicest thing you can ever ask someone, but I'm a little busy."[112]

• Ann B. Davis first became famous as "Schultzy" on *The Bob Cummings Show*, then she became famous to a new generation of fans as Alice on *The Brady Bunch*. A friend once introduced her young daughter to Ms. Davis by saying, "You remember Schultzy." The young daughter indignantly replied, "That's not Schultzy — that's Alice!"[113]

• On *The Dick Van Dyke Show*, Rob and Laura Petrie lived at 448 Bonnie Meadow Road in New Rochelle, New York. This was the real-life address of series creator Carl Reiner — except that he added an extra number to the address so that fans of the series wouldn't stop by and knock on his door.[114]

• Orson Welles was such a huge (pun definitely intended) fan of *The Dick Van Dyke Show* that he once broke off an interview with director Peter Bogdanovich when he realized that a re-run of his favorite sitcom was on TV.[115]

Fathers

• The father of Balanchine ballerina Allegra Kent once appeared on TV's *Gong Show*. He dressed himself as an egg, and he recited some poetry he had written. He spoke eloquently, but every time he mentioned a rifle shot in his poetry, he cracked an egg over his head — this particular poem had lots of rifle shots. Eventually, he was gonged. Some people regarded it as a pitiful performance, but Ms. Kent was proud of her father for developing an offbeat act and for not being afraid to perform his act on TV.[116]

• When comedian Morey Amsterdam appeared on the *Ed Sullivan Show* for the first time, using his cello as a comic prop, his father — a professional cellist — telegraphed him: "YOUR CELLO IS OUT OF TUNE."[117]

Food

• Many people's favorite episode of *The Dick Van Dyke Show* is "It May Look Like a Walnut!" In this episode the Earth is invaded by aliens with no thumbs, an extra eye in the back of their head, and a taste for walnuts. Near the end of this episode, Rob Petrie opens a closet and Laura Petrie, played by Mary Tyler Moore, slides out on top of a huge pile of walnuts. Ms. Moore relates that the week the episode was being filmed, all the members of the cast were snacking on walnuts, which filled them with gas. As Ms. Moore slid down the pile of walnuts, she passed a little gas, but fortunately the sound was covered up by the laughter of the audience.[118]

• On the TV series *Goosebumps*, a dedicated young actress named Kathryn Long played a role that required her to eat a sandwich in which a worm had been placed. Not knowing about the worm, the character takes a bite of the sandwich, chews it, and swallows it. Of course, the people behind the series wanted to use a fake worm for the scene, but being a dedicated young actress, Ms. Long said, "We need a real worm. I can't really play the scene right unless we use a real worm." So they used a real worm, and for the twelve takes it took to shoot the scene right, Ms. Long bit into a real worm, chewed it up, and swallowed it.[119]

• As a teenager, Lucille Ball went to New York to try to get work as an actress and model. Frequently, after running out of money, she would have to come back home, but she kept going back to New York. One way that she survived was by finding "one-doughnut" men. In Lucy's words: "This is a guy who sits at a counter and orders doughnuts and coffee. He drinks his coffee, eats one doughnut and puts down a nickel tip. I'd do a fast slide onto his stool, yell for a cup of coffee, pay for it with his nickel, and eat the other doughnut."[120]

• As a result of playing Laverne in the TV sitcom *Laverne and Shirley* (Cindy Williams played Shirley), Penny Marshall had many interesting experiences. One day, she got some cheesecake out of the refrigerator at home. When her husband asked where the cheesecake had come from, she was able to honestly reply, "A man in a bunny suit gave it to Cindy and me."[121]

• Bernie Fein was the co-creator of TV's *Hogan's Heroes*. He borrowed the name of the lead character, Colonel Robert Hogan, from an actor friend of his, whom he cast in the series' 15th episode. In gratitude, Mr. Hogan shared a real "Hogan's Hero" with Mr. Fein — a 5-foot hero sandwich filled with meats, cheeses, lettuce, tomato, and spices.[122]

Gays and Lesbians

• The TV series *Xena: Warrior Princess* boasted not one, but two, lesbian icons. Lucy Lawless (Xena) and Renee O'Connor (Gabrielle) enjoyed a relationship with a serious lesbian subtext. Attending a convention of *Xena* fans, Ms. Lawless appeared and informed the crowd that Xena had recently been voted the number-two most-loved lesbian icon in the world. She then asked, "Would you like to meet number one?" No fools, the crowd — mostly composed of lesbians — screamed yes, and Ms. O'Connor walked on stage — to more screams. Of course, both Ms. Lawless and Ms. O'Connor have male fans. After Ms. O'Connor's character was voted the number-one most-loved lesbian icon in the world, she posted a message on the WWW thanking all of her female fans for voting for her. A number of male fans wrote back, posting messages that said, "Wait a minute, we voted for you, too!"[123]

• Air America Radio host (and now MSNBC host) Rachel Maddow decided to come out of the closet in a very public way when she was a student at Stanford. In every bathroom in her residence hall, she posted signs announcing that she is a lesbian — by the end of 24 hours everyone in her residence hall knew her sexual orientation. The school newspaper even published an article saying that she was one of the only two out lesbians in the freshman class. Ms. Maddow says, "Funnily enough, only one other person was out, and she was not one of the many girls I was sleeping with."[124]

• Quite a few gay men think that Ira Glass, host of radio's and TV's *This American Life*, is gay. Sometimes, he will mention on air that he has a wife, and a gay man will email him to say, "Please, stop pretending. Who is this 'wife' character you talk about?" Mr. Glass is certainly open to gays. Asked by an *Advocate* interviewer what it felt like to be included among other celebrities who are thought to be gay but who aren't, Mr. Glass replied, "I always feel like it's very flattering to be included in that club. It's a group you'd like to be part of."[125]

• Black comedian Chris Rock had a notable skit on his HBO TV series. A black man and a white man meet each other on a dark street, and the two men are wary, expecting that the other man may do something violent. The men angrily ask each other what the other is doing that late in the neighborhood when suddenly ... the white man grabs the black man and kisses him ... then the black man grabs the white man and kisses him back. The announcer explains, "Gay sex. It's colorblind."[126]

• On *The Hollywood Squares*, gay comedy writer Bruce Vilanch was asked, "You are the most popular fruit in America. What are you?" Bruce got a big laugh when he answered, "Humble." (The other correct answer? "Banana.") Another gay comedian, Paul Lynde, can often be seen on Nick at Nite guest-starring in old sitcoms. When he was on the game show *The Hollywood Squares* long ago, he was asked how long the typical affair lasts — he replied, "About 15 minutes." (The correct answer was about two weeks.)[127]

• During the summer between her junior and senior years of high school, Chastity Bono, the lesbian daughter of Sonny Bono and Cher, was riding her bike in New York City when she came across a Gay Pride parade. Never having heard of such a thing before, she was surprised — and exhilarated. She joined the parade and became one of hundreds of people celebrating their homosexuality.[128]

• Roseanne Conner (a character on TV's *Roseanne*) knows how to treat people. When Sandra Bernhard's lesbian character worried about how the Conner family would have treated her if she had come out of the closet, Roseanne said, "We would have treated you like anyone else around here. We would have mocked you for a while — until we got tired of it — and then we would have dropped it."[129]

• The first lesbian game-show host was probably Hella von Sinnen, who co-hosted *Alles, Nichts, Oder!?* (*All, Nothing, Or!?*) in Germany. While accepting a Bambi award (the equivalent of USAmerica's Emmy award) in 1990, she astonished the audience when she said, "I would like to thank my wife for her support."[130]

• Gay deejay Jeremy Hovies of Sirius OutQ Radio occasionally receives a telephone call from a person who wants to tell him that homosexuals are evil. When that happens, he asks why the caller is so much more concerned about gay sex than he — a gay man — is.[131]

• Gay men can be judgmental. An overweight TV sitcom star once participated in a Hollywood Christmas parade that was televised. As she rode down Hollywood Boulevard, many gay men greeted her by shouting, "Lose some weight, b*tch!"[132]

• Chastity Bono, the daughter of Sonny Bono and Cher, was still a teenager when she said to her best friend, "Gina, I have something to tell you. I think I'm gay." Gina's reaction was excellent — she shrugged, then said, "What's the big deal?"[133]

• Lesbian humorist Ellen Orleans once attended a National Lesbian Conference in Atlanta. When she was there, someone posted this sign: "*L.A. Law* update: Abby asked C.J. for a date. C.J. said yes!!!!"[134]

Good Deeds

• During the late 1950s, John F. Kennedy and Robert Kennedy worked together on the Senate Investigations Subcommittee, and they appeared on its televised hearings. After seeing them on TV, Kathleen Ann Corley, an 8th-grade student in Chicago, decided to write them and ask for autographed photographs. She sent her letter to John F. Kennedy, although it was addressed to both brothers. He quickly sent her both a letter and an autographed photograph, then he gave the letter to his brother Bobby, who also sent her both a letter and an autographed photograph.[135]

• Oprah Winfrey is considerate and knows how to give good gifts. The executive producer of her TV talk show (and a close friend) was Debra Di Maio. Ms. Winfrey once gave her the all-expenses-paid gift of dinner with her friends — one dinner a month for a year, in various exciting cities around the world![136]

Hosts

• Ed Sullivan could be a good man to work for. For one thing, he was a good editor. If a comic routine needed to be shortened, he could tell the comedian where it should be cut. Once, Shelley Berman performed a comic routine that ran 12 minutes in rehearsal. After rehearsal, he received a call to see Mr. Sullivan. He expected that the sketch would need to be shortened, but Mr. Sullivan instead suggested that a line be added. That night, when he performed the sketch live on TV, Mr. Berman noticed a change in lights, and the addition of violin music, both of which enhanced the poignant tone he set in the second half of the sketch. And when he went backstage following his live performance, a telephone call was waiting for him — Mr. Sullivan's wife had called to congratulate him on his performance.[137]

• Before becoming famous as the host of *Late Night* on NBC and the *Late Show* on CBS, David Letterman appeared on television in his native Indiana. Among other duties, Mr. Letterman hosted late-night movies in a program he named *Freeze-Dried Movies*. During what was really his second week of hosting the show, Mr. Letterman celebrated what he called his "10th anniversary" as host.[138]

Husbands and Wives

• Vicki Lawrence starred on *The Carol Burnett Show* and *Mama's Family* for years, but fans sometimes mistake her for either Carol Burnett or Carol Lawrence, an actress who was married for a while to singer Robert Goulet. Once, she was guesting on *Password*, and at one point, members of the audience were allowed to ask the celebrity contestants a question. A woman asked Vicki, "Carol, what was it like being married to Robert Goulet?" Vicki decided to answer the question, even though it was obvious that the woman had confused her with Carol Lawrence: "He was a total son of a b*tch, and I divorced his *ss." The woman in the audience was shocked, but *Password* host Allen Ludden nearly peed his pants laughing. A little later, Vicki was at a party, and the real Carol Lawrence was present. Vicki was afraid that she would be angry, but Ms. Lawrence told her, "I heard about *Password* — you took the words right out of my mouth."[139]

• In the 1970s, James Garner and Mariette Hartley made a series of TV commercials for Polaroid in which they appeared to be a feisty, but happily married, couple. The actors were so good that many viewers thought they were actually married. Ms. Hartley even started wearing a T-shirt that said, "I am not Mrs. James Garner." Meanwhile, the real Mrs. James Garner started wearing a T-shirt that said, "I am Mrs. James Garner."[140]

• Bea Wain and Andre Baruch were the husband-and-wife stars of a radio show. Mr. Wain once said on the air, "The hen that laid double-yolk eggs will be exhibited at the New York State Fair. However, due to the excessive heat, the hen hasn't laid since last Monday." His wife added, "That could happen to any of us."[141]

• After Trigger, the horse of TV and movie star Roy Rogers, died, Mr. Rogers had him stuffed. His wife, Dale Evans, told him, "Roy, don't you go getting any ideas about me."[142]

Language

• While living in Italy, actress Eve Arden rented a villa from a Marchese. While living in the villa, she kept track of all the drinking glasses her family had broken so that she could pay for them at the end of her lease. However, because of her poor Italian, the Marchese got a shock because he thought that the glass she was reporting on was window glass ("vietro") instead of drinking glasses ("bicchieri"). "My God," he said (in Italian) after hearing her report on the telephone, "there can't be a windowpane left in the place!"[143]

• In the TV series *Hogan's Heroes*, extras frequently had to speak a little German because the series was set in a World War II prisoner-of-war camp (not in a concentration camp). Chris Anders once played a German guard who had to tell some trucks to take off, so he said, "Fahrt Los." However, because the German word "fahrt" sounds like the English word "fart," the director stopped the scene, saying, "We can't use that!"[144]

• Robin Williams' humor could be crude. Before a *Comic Relief* show, members of the production staff created a pool in which they guessed how long it would take for Mr. Williams to make a penis joke in the show, which started at 6 p.m. The winner guessed 6:07 p.m. (Mr. Williams might have made the joke even sooner, but the opening number of *Comic Relief* took five minutes.)[145]

• After Honor Blackman, who played Cathy Gale, left the 1960s tongue-in-cheek TV spy series *The Avengers*, her partner in the series, John Steed, played by Patrick Macnee, said in an episode, "I've no doubt that she is pussy-footing around on some island." (Ms. Blackman left *The Avengers* to play the character Pussy Galore in the James Bond movie *Goldfinger*.)[146]

• In the early days of radio, Jan Savitt was the leader of a house orchestra. One day, he decided to fire George, his Polish secretary, who was in charge of all the orchestra's files and records. Very quickly, however, Mr. Savitt had to rehire George. George had kept all of the orchestra's files and records in Polish.[147]

• The star of the TV series *Buffy the Vampire Slayer*, Sarah Michelle Gellar, collects first editions of children's books, including *Alice in Wonderland* and *Peter Pan*. She is especially fond of the author Dr. Seuss because in his book *There's a Wocket in My Pocket*, he wrote the line "There's a Gellar in the cellar."[148]

• Jeff Stone, an outfielder for the Boston Red Sox, once played for a while in Latin America, and when he returned to the United States, he left his TV behind. Why? He explained, "All the programs were in Spanish."[149]

• To break the ice with her normal-hearing co-stars on the TV series *Reasonable Doubts*, deaf actress Marlee Matlin taught them how to say dirty words in sign language.[150]

Chapter 4: From Live Television to Prejudice

Live Television

• Cliff Robertson stayed true to the character of Charlie Gordon, the main character of Daniel Keyes' story "Flowers for Algernon." In the story, a mentally retarded man undergoes a medical procedure that makes him a genius for a while before he slips back into mental retardation. Of course, that ending is powerful, and of course, many Hollywood types wished to change that ending to a sappy ending in which Charlie retains his genius. In the television version (before the later movie version), Cliff Robertson was supposed to look at a copy of *Paradise Lost*, which the character Charlie had lost the ability to read, and then act surprised — as if he could read it and his genius ability was returning. However, when the time came, despite orders to make the ending happy, Mr. Robertson played the scene without the sappiness. And since the television version — on *The U.S. Steel Hour* — was live, no one could make him re-shoot the scene. (Of course, Mr. Robertson was told that he would never work on TV again, but after rave reviews and an Emmy nomination poured in, he started hearing congratulations, not threats.)[151]

• The very first guest of Edward R. Murrow's live TV show *Person to Person* was Dodger catcher Roy Campanella. The show debuted on Saturday, Oct. 2, 1953, the day that the Dodgers were playing in the third game of the World Series. Following a rehearsal that Friday, Mr. Murrow joked, "All you have to do, Roy, is hit a home run tomorrow and then come on in my first show." That Saturday, in the eighth inning, when the score was a 2-2 tie, Mr. Campanella hit a home run to drive in the winning run. His appearance on *Person to Person* made an impressive debut for what turned out to be a long-running TV series.[152]

• On live TV, mistakes did happen. For example, in the "Better Living Through TV" episode of *The Honeymooners*, Jackie Gleason plays the Chef of the Future while advertising a modern gizmo on TV. At the end of the scene, Jackie accidentally hit a flat that had been painted to represent a wall. The "wall" fell down, Jackie fell down, then Ed Norton (played by Art Carney) fell down, and today you can view the whole scene during the re-runs. Even the accidents were recorded when you were doing live TV. Fortunately, the audience thought the accident was hilarious.[153]

Meetings

• In 1971, David Davis and Lorenzo Music were asked to present an idea for a new TV series at CBS. When they met with CBS executive Alan Wagner, Mr. Music remembers, "We said that our idea was — that we didn't have an idea." Mr. Wagner replied, "I like it — tell me more." This was a wise answer, for Mr. Davis and Mr. Music created *The Bob Newhart Show*.[154]

• Carl Reiner, George Shapiro, and Allan Burns once held a meeting in a sauna, where of course they were naked and dripping with sweat. Mr. Reiner came up with a brilliant idea, and filled with enthusiasm, Mr. Shapiro turned to Mr. Burns and said, "Write that down!" Mr. Burns replied, "With what — sweat?"[155]

Mishaps

• In the early days of television, Paul Ritts directed a program about dogs on a local station. He recognized that he had a problem even before the program aired — live — because the man who would host the program frequently used the word "bitch" to refer to female dogs. In fact, the program host was hard of hearing, so he spoke loudly — so loudly that during the course of their meeting Mr. Ritts received a telephone call from a female employee complaining about the language coming from Mr. Ritts' office. Of course, Mr. Ritts explained to the TV host that broadcast standards would not permit the use of the word "bitch" on the air, and the TV host promised to try to restrain himself.

And so he did, although during rehearsal he said "bit ... female" twice and "bitch" three times. Fortunately, during the live broadcast he didn't use the words "bitch" or "bit ... female" at all. Unfortunately, during the live broadcast, a large dog bit one of the cameramen, and TV viewers at home saw the cameraman walking across the stage while dragging the dog — which still had its teeth in his leg. The cameraman was also yelling — "SON OF A B*TCH!"[156]

• James Van Der Beek, star of TV's *Dawson's Creek*, got into acting partly through an accident. When he was 13 years old, he played organized football, but he suffered a concussion in a game. Instead of sitting on the bench the rest of the season, he decided to try acting in community theater and landed the role of bad boy Danny Zuko in *Grease*. That role increased his interest in acting, and soon he was heading to New York City to try to land roles. He did get a role in an acne-medicine commercial in which he would play the teenager with clear skin. Unfortunately, on the day the commercial was shot James had an outbreak of zits. Fortunately, he was able to keep the job — the zits were covered up with lots of makeup. Acting as a teenager had one other bad result for James: At Cheshire Academy, he had been elected vice president of his class, but he missed too many meetings because he was filming a movie titled *Angus*, and so he was impeached.[157]

• Comedian Dave Thomas once starred in a television series titled *The Dave Thomas Comedy Show*. On the very first show, Mr. Thomas and guest Chevy Chase did a sketch about being afraid to fly, and they even wore ridiculous wigs with hair standing straight on end to show how scared of flying they were. On the night the TV show debuted, Mr. Thomas invited Mr. Chase and many other friends to his house, and they sat watching the program. Unfortunately, breaking news occurred as the fear-of-flying sketch unfolded. A real airplane crashed, and news of the crash — and film of staggering survivors — kept interrupting the show. For a while, the TV station alternated between showing horrible airplane wreckage and showing Mr. Thomas and Mr. Chase in ridiculous wigs joking about airplane disasters. Shortly afterward, the series was cancelled.[158]

• Back in 1967, a TV commercial for Colt 45 Malt Liquor showed an impassive man named Billy Van seated at a table in a bullring as a matador fights a bull. The bull charged Mr. Van and the table, crashing him into a wall. In a close-up, Mr. Van dusts himself off impassively, sits down at the table impassively, and pours himself a glass of Colt 45 Malt Liquor — which makes him smile. The stunt with the bull was unplanned — the bull was supposed to ignore the man at the table and concentrate instead on the matador fighting him. Actually, the man at the table was not Mr. Van; it was another matador dressed as Mr. Van, who appeared only in the close-ups. The owner of the bullring told the TV film crew, "Don't worry. If de matador dies, I get you another one." Fortunately, the matador did not die.[159]

• Carole Lombard once appeared in a radio program sponsored by International Silver. In addition to performing on the program, Ms. Lombard read a commercial endorsing the sponsor's products. The commercial touted International Silver's new pattern of silverware, Interlude, and Ms. Lombard had to read, "The bride who has Interlude on her dining room table will want Interlude in every room of the house." However, during a dress rehearsal, a practical joker changed the wording of the commercial, so that Ms. Lombard found herself reading, "The bride who has Intercourse on her dining room table will want Intercourse in every room of the house."[160]

• Art Linkletter once pulled a stunt on his *People are Funny* TV program in which he rented a room at a hotel and had a young woman drop notes into the street reading, "Am being held by kidnappers in Room 617 ... Help!" Sure enough, a sailor saw one of the notes and came rushing into the hotel, where he "rescued" the young woman, then appeared on Mr. Linkletter's TV show. Unfortunately, several of the notes that the young woman dropped from her window fell to a ledge, where they stayed until a few days later, when they were blown into the street. Eventually, police officers rushed into room 617, searching for kidnappers and startling the paying guest.[161]

• Arthur O'Connell once had the pleasure of conducting for Lily Pons — and of conducting a few selections without Ms. Pons. After Ms. Pons' final song, the MC announced, "And now the Philadelphia Orchestra will play Beethoven's *Consecration of the House* under the direction of Mr. O'Connell." Unfortunately, a loud member of the audience yelled — with a voice clearly audible to Mr. O'Connell and the millions of people listening on the radio — "To h*ll with Mr. O'Connell; give us some more Lily Pons!" Ms. Pons was enough of a lady not to laugh — until she saw Mr. O'Connell laughing.[162]

• George Burns and Gracie Allen had years of experience performing in vaudeville before they started doing their radio show. This long experience came in handy when mishaps occurred on their show. One day, the lights in the studio went out, and no one could read the script. On another occasion, Gracie accidentally dropped her script, and the pages scattered everywhere. Both times, they ignored the script. George simply asked, "Gracie, how's your brother?" — and Gracie started one of their well-memorized and very funny vaudeville routines.[163]

• Archeologist Brian Rose lectured in 1996 at Ohio University, where he told this story about excavating the site of Troy in Turkey: At the site is a huge wooden horse that was built by the BBC for a documentary on the Trojan War. Today the horse is a tourist attraction, as people can go inside the horse and look out through shuttered windows. One day, members of Mr. Rose's crew were inside the Trojan horse smoking with the shutters closed. This alarmed the Turkish security guards because they noticed smoke coming out of the horse's nostrils.[164]

• British broadcaster Magnus Magnusson once invited some archeologists to appear on his television program because they had discovered evidence that the headquarters of the Roman fleet in Britain

(*Classis Britannicus*) had been located at Dover. The most important evidence they had found was a red slate marked with the Roman initials "C.B." The archeologists brought the red slate with them and handed it to Mr. Magnusson, who promptly dropped it, breaking it in two, in between the initials.[165]

• While working as a co-anchor at WJZ-TV in Baltimore, Maryland, Oprah Winfrey ran into problems when the assistant news director decided to change Ms. Winfrey's appearance. Ms. Winfrey went to a beauty parlor and got a permanent, but it made all of her hair fall out. She was totally bald! Worse, she couldn't find a wig that fit while her hair grew back, so she was forced to wear scarves. She said, "All my self-esteem was gone. My whole self-image. I cried constantly."[166]

• Ralph Edwards used to surprise celebrities on his TV show, *This is Your Life*, in which he would bring on friends and family of the celebrity to reminisce about the celebrity's life. Many celebrities — but not all — enjoyed this. Newsman Lowell Thomas was one who did not. On air, he referred to the proceedings as "a sinister conspiracy." When Mr. Edwards said to him, "Lowell, I know you are going to enjoy tonight's surprise," an irritated Mr. Thomas replied, "I doubt it."[167]

• In one episode of *The Dick Van Dyke Show*, Mary Tyler Moore (who played Laura Petrie) was required to make some eggs. The scene was supposed to last five minutes, but unfortunately the actors worked faster than that, and when the eggs were supposed to be done, they were runny. According to Ms. Moore, "It was quite a problem — what I really needed was a soup bowl! But Dick ate them, bless him, and only turned a little green."[168]

• The first episode of *The Simpsons* was supposed to air on Fox in the fall of 1989, but it was delayed because its executive producers — Matt Groening, James L. Brooks, and Sam Simon — discovered that the first episode contained several unauthorized tasteless jokes. (Apparently, authorized tasteless jokes are OK.) *The Simpsons* premiered as a Christmas special in 1989, and the actual series started in January 1990.[169]

• Tracey Ullman is a comedian who is known for her ability to create characters with her incredible acting talent and the aid of costumes, wigs, rubber masks, etc. While filming *The Tracey Ullman Show* for the Fox network, she changed characters so often that she once passed out in her dressing room from accidentally inhaling the chemicals used to remove her makeup.[170]

• Kristen Bell, star of the TV series *Veronica Mars*, says that she once "fell madly in love" with *Saturday Night Live* star Amy Poehler because of her petiteness and sense of comedy. On a red carpet, she saw Ms. Poehler's then-husband, actor Will Arnett, and told him, "I'm absolutely in love with your wife." He replied, "I'm so glad you didn't say me. That would have been awkward."[171]

• Honor Blackman starred on *The Avengers* for a couple of years, then left the TV series in order to star as the character Pussy Galore in the James Bond movie *Goldfinger*. While she was on a promotional tour for the movie, she appeared on KGO-TV, where an interviewer told her, "I've covered topless bathing suits, bottomless bathing suits, and now I've got Pussy Galore!"[172]

• Julia Child is my kind of cook — very good, but slightly frazzled. One day, while she was cooking on TV, some of the ingredients fell to the floor. She told her TV audience, "If this happens, just scoop it back. Remember, you are alone in the kitchen, and nobody can see you."[173]

Money

• Jack Paar and Ed Sullivan used to compete for the same guests. Mr. Sullivan paid anywhere from $5,000 to $7,500 for an appearance, while Mr. Paar's *Tonight Show* could afford to pay only $320. In an attempt to keep performers from appearing with Mr. Paar, Mr. Sullivan announced that anyone who appeared on *The Tonight Show* would be paid only $320 for appearing on his show. Of course, many entertainers canceled their appearances on Mr. Paar's show. However, one entertainer who remained loyal to Mr. Paar was comedian Joey Bishop, who joked on *The Tonight Show*, "I have one gripe. You told me Sullivan paid only $80. I thought this was the big money."[174]

• In November of 2007 Hollywood writers went on strike. Why? Ken Levine gave an answer in a column that he wrote for the *Toronto Star*. He pointed out that he had recently received a check from American Airlines, which had been showing episodes that he had written for *Becker*, *Cheers*, and *M*A*S*H* and that he had directed for *Dharma & Greg*, *Everybody Loves Raymond*, and *Frasier*. He estimates, based on number of years and on number of flights, that American Airlines has shown these episodes 10,000 times. So how much was Mr. Levine's check for? Nineteen cents.[175]

• In the early days of radio, singers often did not know how much to charge. Because they charged usually by the size of the audience at concerts — a smaller fee at smaller concert halls, and a larger fee at larger concert halls — they thought that they should charge a lot because of the vast size of the radio audience. Opera singer Harold Williams was once asked by Stanton Jefferies what he would charge for a radio broadcast. He said 100 guineas. Mr. Jefferies replied, "We had in mind seven guineas." (Of course, the radio audience did not pay admission the way the audience at a concert hall would.)[176]

• When Wah Ming Chang and Gene Warren decided to close their firm Project Unlimited, which had created special effects for such television series as *Star Trek* and such movies as *The Time Machine*, they advertised an auction of the models and costumes they had created. Bidding was fierce as sci-fi fans acquired memorabilia of their favorite shows, so Mr. Chang and Mr. Warren went to the back and dug through the trash bins to find worn-out puppets and other items that they had been about to throw out, but which collectors eagerly purchased.[177]

• When she was a young woman, Oprah Winfrey entered a beauty contest that she did not expect to win. However, the judges found her answers to their questions original and interesting. For example, the final question asked of the three finalists was, "What would you do if you had one million dollars?" The first two finalists gave unoriginal, uninteresting answers — one would use the money to help her family, and the other would use it to help the poor. Ms. Winfrey's answer was, "If I had a million dollars, I'd be a spending fool!" She won.[178]

• Charles Correll and Freeman Gosden created and played the roles of Amos 'n' Andy. Early in their career, they were asked to come to a meeting to discuss a radio program that they might star in. Mr. Correll and Mr. Gosden discussed how much to ask for their salary ahead of time, and they decided that they would be lucky to get $10 a week apiece. Therefore, when they were asked what salary they wanted — and then quickly were offered $125 a week — they sputtered, "Ten — ten — tentatively, yes."[179]

• In the 1960s, Ernie Anderson played wild-and-crazy horror-show host Ghoulardi in Cleveland, Ohio. After quitting, he moved to Los Angeles, California, where he made big money as a TV announcer. One day, he and his friend Linn Sheldon walked into a studio, where Mr. Sheldon lit a cigarette. Before Mr. Sheldon had finished smoking the cigarette, Mr. Anderson had read four TV promotional spots and made $30,000.[180]

• Comedian Soupy Sales used to collect portraits of United States Presidents and American founding fathers. On his TV show for children, he once told his young viewers to go through Mommy's purse and Daddy's wallet and mail him "the little green pieces of paper with pictures of George Washington, Benjamin Franklin, Lincoln, and Jefferson on them." In return, he promised to send the children a postcard from Puerto Rico.[181]

• The British tongue-in-cheek spy series *The Avengers* was definitely capitalistic. It even had an Exploitation Manager whose job was to sell product placements — if you had a product you wanted to appear on the series, this was the person you had to deal with.[182]

Music

• Ron Sweed, aka the Ghoul, hosted several mostly bad movies on a television program airing in Cleveland, Ohio, during the 1970s and 1980s. The Ghoul tended to show the same bad movies over and over because the station bought the rights to very few movies. To keep things interesting, The Ghoul used to change the sound tracks. For example, an actress in *Attack of the Mushroom People* sang a song on a cruise ship. The Ghoul disliked the song, so when she sang, he dubbed in "Gypsies, Tramps, and Thieves" or "Who Stole the Kishka" or some other song instead. And when a disembodied head babbled in *The Brain That Wouldn't Die*, he played a song whose lyrics went "PAPA-OOM-MOW-MOW."[183]

• Early in his career, following a radio broadcast in 1936, Robert Irwin received a fan letter from famed tenor John McCormack. The following year, the non-music firm for which Mr. Irwin worked booked a recital at which Mr. McCormack would sing, and Mr. Irwin was present — although he had not yet met and been introduced to Mr. McCormack — at a press conference which had been arranged for the famed tenor. A newspaper writer asked Mr. McCormack whether any of Ireland's younger singers were promising in particular. He replied, "Well, there's a young fella called Irwin ...." Of course, the two were introduced immediately, and Mr. McCormack became Mr. Irwin's mentor.[184]

Police

• As a child attending the Peninsula School of Creative Education in Menlo Park, California, Wah Ming Chang and his friend Torben Deirup created a life-sized dummy that they used in practical jokes. Once they placed the dummy in a gutter, then hid across the street and watched as some people came out of their house, looked at the realistic dummy, then ran back into their house to call the police. Wah and Torben removed the dummy without being seen, and the neighbors had some explaining to do when the police came. Later, after playing several more practical jokes, Wah and Torben were caught red-handed with the dummy. A police officer sternly told them that if their dummy ever appeared in a gutter again, they would be attending reform school. As an adult, Mr. Chang became an artist and a special-effects wizard for the TV series *Star Trek*.[185]

• Before starring as the lead actor in TV's *Hogan's Heroes*, Bob Crane was a well-known disk jockey in Connecticut. Because he was a celebrity, police officers in Connecticut sometimes let him go with a warning (and no ticket) when he was caught speeding. When Mr. Crane moved to California, he wanted to continue receiving favors, so he wrote on the back of his driver's license, "I am a radio star," where any police officer who stopped him would be sure to see it. Sure enough, he was stopped for speeding, but this time the police officer wrote him a ticket. Across the top of the ticket was written this note: "I am a police officer."[186]

• When Will Smith was starring in *The Fresh Prince of Bel-Air*, one episode revolved around his character driving around in an expensive car and being stopped by the police because they think it is suspicious for a black man to drive such an expensive car. This episode was based on Mr. Smith's real life — often the police stopped him because they thought it was suspicious for him to drive such an expensive car.[187]

• Pianist Oscar Levant once avoided a speeding ticket because he was listening to Beethoven on his car radio. He told the police officer, "You can't possibly hear the last movement of Beethoven's Seventh, and go slow."[188]

Politics

• George Jessel once made a speech on radio in support of the campaign of Franklin D. Roosevelt for President. The other speakers went over their time limits, so Mr. Jessel's speech had to be quite short. He told the audience, "Ladies and gentlemen, most of my eloquent colleagues have this evening taken up ever so much of their time in expounding the weaknesses and vices of President Roosevelt's opponent, Thomas Dewey. I shall not and I could not do this. I know Governor Thomas E. Dewey, and Mr. Dewey is a fine man." As it is not the custom to praise the opponent in politics, a hush fell over the Roosevelt supporters — until Mr. Jessel added, "Yes, Mr. Dewey is a fine man. So is my Uncle Morris. My Uncle Morris shouldn't be President; neither should Dewey."[189]

• Carol Burnett became very successful in New York City, both on Broadway and on television. She was a hit in her first appearance on *The Ed Sullivan Show* on August 11, 1957, when she sang the comic song "I Made a Fool of Myself Over John Foster Dulles." (In real life, Ms. Burnett and Mr. Dulles had never met.) The following Sunday, Mr. Dulles, who was Secretary of State from 1953 to 1959, appeared on *Meet the Press*. At the end of the program, a reporter asked Mr. Dulles a light-hearted question about his relationship with the young woman who had sang about him on *The Ed Sullivan Show*. Mr. Dulles smiled and replied, "I make it a point never to discuss affairs of the heart in public."[190]

• Politicians have long been aware of the all-seeing eye of television. During the Army-McCarthy hearings, Senator Joseph McCarthy wrote a note asking the television camera operators to point their cameras at someone else for a while so that he could blow his nose.[191]

Popularity

• The 1950s situation comedy *I Love Lucy* was amazingly popular when it appeared originally on Monday. In fact, it was so popular that Marshall Fields department store decided to close on Monday nights, and so it put up this sign: "We love Lucy, too, so we're closing on Monday nights."[192]

• The television show *I Love Lucy* is aptly named. Presidential candidate Adlai Stevenson, who was running against Dwight David Eisenhower, once pre-empted an episode of *I Love Lucy*, and hate mail poured in to the candidate. One viewer wrote: "I love Lucy. I like Ike. Drop dead."[193]

Practical Jokes

• In junior high school, Jay Leno used to create havoc in the classroom whenever a substitute teacher appeared on the scene. For example, a classmate named Lewis Trumbore used to help him fake a suicide. Lewis would hold Jay's shoes outside a window, then yell for the teacher and say, "Come here, quick! Jay Leno's hanging out this window! I can't hold on much longer!" Then he would drop the shoes, the other students — who were in on the joke — would scream, and the teacher would look out the window to see Jay lying motionless on the ground. Of course, he hadn't jumped — he was just playing dead.[194]

• When he was still working for NBC, *Late Night* talk-show host David Letterman looked out of his office window and noticed *Today Show* talk-show host Bryant Gumbel filming an interview outside. David being David, he got a bullhorn and shouted down to Mr. Gumbel: "My name is Larry Grossman, I am the president of NBC News — and I'm not wearing any pants." The interruption ruined Mr. Gumbel's interview, and he had to film it again, but *Late Night* fans enjoyed a good laugh.[195]

• Actress Betty White has been on television seemingly forever — and she has had fun doing it. In an early series, *Life With Elizabeth*, she starred with Del Moore, who enjoyed playing a trick on the director. Between takes, he used to slip his ring off one hand and put it on his other hand. When an episode aired, he and Betty White used to enjoy watching his ring magically jump from one hand to the other.[196]

• After *Richard Diamond, Private Eye*, Mary Tyler Moore went on to *The Dick Van Dyke Show*. In real life Ms. Moore never made a secret of her dislike for housework, although she was playing Laura Petrie, a near-perfect homemaker. At a party Ms. Moore and her husband gave for her co-workers, Mr. Van Dyke wrote in the dust on top of her refrigerator, "Needs Soap."[197]

Prejudice

• Sheldon Leonard was the producer of *I Spy* in the days when few African-Americans were on TV. He wanted to hire the young black comic Bill Cosby to co-star with Robert Culp, but he worried about whether the NBC network brass would approve the deal. So Mr. Leonard armed himself with arguments why signing Mr. Cosby would not alienate the TV audience, then he went to see NBC President Robert Kintner. He told Mr. Kintner that he had in mind a young comic to co-star with Mr. Culp, but that he hadn't signed him yet. When Mr. Kintner asked why not, Mr. Leonard replied, "Because he's black." Mr. Kintner then asked, "What difference does that make?" Relieved, Mr. Leonard said, "As of this moment, Mr. Kintner, it makes no difference whatsoever."[198]

• Gay deejay John McMullen of Sirius OutQ Radio occasionally visited the late famous homophobe Fred Phelps in Mr. Phelps' native Topeka, Kansas. One day, while traveling from San Francisco to New York, Mr. McMullen even turned a half-hour, live-radio visit with Mr. Phelps into a fundraiser, telling his audience that he was taking a Sodom to Gomorrah via Topeka Tour and raising several thousand dollars for a charity that Mr. Phelps did NOT support: the Matthew Shepard Foundation.[199]

• George Takei, who played Mr. Hikaru Sulu on the original *Star Trek* TV series, grew up in American internment camps for Japanese-Americans during World War II. He had a teacher who referred to him as "that little Jap boy," and each morning, he was able to look out the school window and see barbed-wire fences and guard towers as he ended the Pledge of Allegiance by reciting "with justice and liberty for all."[200]

Chapter 5: From Problem-Solving to Writers

Problem-Solving

• The opening credits and the exterior shots of early episodes of *The Mary Tyler Moore Show* feature a beautiful Victorian house where the characters Mary Richards, Rhoda Morgenstern, and Phyllis Lindstrom are supposed to live. The house really belonged to a humanities professor at the University of Minnesota. Unfortunately, after the series became popular, tourists began to ring her doorbell, then ask to meet Mary. When the MTM production crew arrived to take more exterior shots of the house, the professor declined to give them permission, but they started to take the shots anyway. The professor stopped them by hanging a banner outside Mary Richards' window. The banner made a demand about a then-current political situation: "IMPEACH NIXON." In later episodes, Mary Richards moved to a high-rise apartment house.[201]

• This is a story that the late central Ohio sportscaster Jimmy Crum liked to tell: Paul Robinson played for the Cleveland Browns under coach Paul Brown. Once he scored a 55-yard touchdown, but instead of heading straight for the goal line, he ran to the other side of the field, then headed for the goal line. When Mr. Brown asked him later why he had run to the other side of the field, Mr. Robinson explained, "Coach, this game is being televised nationally and my folks are watching. The cameras are over on that side of the field, and I knew they'd see me better if I ran over there." By the way, according to weatherman Jym Ganahl of Channel 4 News in Columbus, Ohio, Mr. Crum used to eat a dozen White Castle hamburgers for breakfast each morning.[202]

• As a young actress newly arrived in New York City, Carol Burnett ran into a problem. She couldn't get an acting job because she had no experience, and she couldn't get experience because no one would give her an acting job. She solved the problem by putting on a show with the other young entertainers in her rooming house, which was known as the Rehearsal Club. It worked. Carol and some of the other entertainers got jobs as a result of the *Rehearsal Club Revue*.[203]

• Carroll O'Connor, who played Archie Bunker on *All in the Family*, was a tough negotiator, but so was Norman Lear, who produced the series. According to rumor, whenever Mr. O'Connor didn't want to do something on the series that Mr. Lear really wanted him to do, Mr. Lear would show him a special script titled "The Death of Archie Bunker." Because Mr. O'Connor wanted to continue to do the series, he would agree to do what Mr. Lear wanted him to do.[204]

• Nicholas Colasanto played the role of Ernie "Coach" Pantusso on *Cheers*. Because he was getting older, he had a hard time remembering his lines, but he found ways to cope. For example, he would write his lines on the stage walls and stage furniture. In fact, says *Cheers* co-creator Les Charles, "If you go into the storage room today and find the old set from *Cheers*, you can still see Nick's handwriting on walls and chairs."[205]

• African-American comedian Jimmie Walker was drafted, but he didn't want to fight in the Vietnam War. He was very thin, so he didn't pass the physical, but he was told to gain weight and come back in a few weeks. For the next few weeks, Mr. Walker played basketball in the hot summer sun while wearing a sweatshirt. He then reported for another physical — and beat the draft.[206]

• In the British tongue-in-cheek TV series *The Avengers,* John Steed, played by Patrick Macnee, was an expert in espionage and counter-espionage, although these activities were the domain of two separate government departments: M15 and M16. No problem. The producers of *The Avengers* simply made John Steed an employee of Department M15 and a half.[207]

• Breaking into show business can be difficult, but Peter Sellers found an original way of getting a job with BBC Radio. He telephoned a senior BBC producer, then imitated a famous star named Kenneth Horne. The BBC producer heard what seemed to be the voice of Mr. Horne extravagantly praising the then-unknown comedian Peter Sellers.[208]

Quiz Shows

• John Coveney was an artists' relations manager, and he participated in the quiz segments of the Metropolitan Opera radio broadcasts. Mr. Coveney was known for his quick wit. For example, when he was asked what he most liked about the new house for the Met, he answered, "Not seating latecomers." And when he was asked what he least liked about the Met, he answered, "Not being able to get to my seat when I'm late."[209]

• Ava Gardner once appeared on a TV quiz show while she was having problems in her marriage to Frank Sinatra. She was asked, "Are you married?" After answering this question, she was asked, "Are you glad?" This question was followed by a full minute of silence.[210]

Rehearsals

• Audrey Meadows is famous as Alice Kramdon, wife of Ralph Kramdon, brought to life by Jackie Gleason on *The Honeymooners*. An actress of the theater, Ms. Meadows was used to many and long rehearsals — something Jackie hated because he felt comedic material ought not to be over-rehearsed. According to Jackie, more than one rehearsal was over-rehearsal. In a *TV Guide* article, quoted in Vince Waldron's *Classic Sitcoms*, Ms. Meadows said, "I felt totally unprepared and desperate. Standing in the wings, ready to go on, I'd tell him, 'You are a simply dreadful man.'"[211]

• Early in his career, comedian Don Rickles guest-starred on *The Andy Griffith Show*. Of course, he was eager to do well alongside such established stars as Mr. Griffith and Don Knotts. They rehearsed for most of an afternoon, and finally Mr. Griffith said, "Well, I think we've rehearsed enough. Let's go home." Mr. Rickles pleaded, "No, let's rehearse some more. You guys have millions of feet of film. All I've got are home movies of me and my cousin on a swing."[212]

Religion

• Actress Robia LaMorte, known for her role as Jenny Calendar on TV's *Buffy the Vampire Slayer*, became a born-again Christian after praying for a sign while driving her car on a freeway: "OK, God, you know I believe in You, but I don't get the whole Jesus / born-again Christian thing. If Jesus really is the way, then you need to show me. If you make it clear to me in a way that I can relate to and understand, then I'll check it out." Immediately after she prayed, her car was surrounded by a group of bikers that at first made her think of the Hell's Angels — until she noticed that the jackets the bikers were wearing had crosses on the back — along with the words "We Ride For Jesus." She says that becoming a Christian is the best decision she has ever made.[213]

• Billy Graham occasionally appeared on *The Tonight Show* with Jack Paar, for which he was criticized by people who felt that preachers should not know celebrities. However, Mr. Graham said that Jesus went among the sinners and therefore he could go on Jack Paar's show.[214]

Respect

• NBC News Washington correspondent John Yang is highly respected, very traveled, and completely gay. He could pass as straight, but he chooses not to, saying, "There are certain things about myself that are immutable, and some of them are obvious. I'm Asian. I mean, anyone who sees me on the air or hears my last name knows that. And in a way, I felt that I can't pass as not being Asian, so why should I pass as being straight?" Many conservative politicians really don't care if someone is gay, although you may not be able to tell that from their public pronouncements. After a conservative Republican Senator (unfortunately, not named) read an article in which Mr. Yang's sexual orientation was mentioned, he called Mr. Yang and said, "John, I saw that thing about you in the magazine. I just want to tell you it doesn't make any difference to me. You're still the best d*mned reporter I've ever dealt with." The senator then asked, "I haven't said anything wrong, have I?" Mr. Yang replied, "No, Senator. You said just the right thing."[215]

• Marti Noxon was extremely happy when she got a job writing for the first season of the TV series *Buffy the Vampire Slayer*, a midseason replacement series on the WB — a network that was then pretty much at the bottom of the TV barrel. Of course, shaking with excitement and happiness, she called her mother to give her the good news, but after she said the names of the series and the network, her mother paused, then said, "Oh, honey, next year you'll do better." Another person who didn't get much respect was Sarah Michelle Gellar, who starred as Buffy. She told all her friends about her new role, but they weren't impressed. Ms. Gellar said, "You try being on a midseason replacement show on the WB called *Buffy the Vampire Slayer* and see how much respect you get." Fortunately, as everyone knows, the series became a cult favorite and stayed on the air for seven seasons.[216]

Soap Operas

• Madeleine L'Engle, author of *A Wrinkle in Time*, and Hugh Franklin, a professional actor who played a leading role on the TV soap opera *All My Children*, were happily married for many years. Ms. L'Engle once talked to a taxi driver and speculated about whether her and her husband's many years of marriage had set a record for the longest-lasting marriage between an author and an actor. The taxi driver turned to her and said, "Lady, that's not a record — that's a miracle!"[217]

• During the Great Depression, radio shows of every kind were very popular. Women, of course, enjoyed the soap operas of the day, including *Our Gal Sunday*. In fact, women could walk around the block in New York City in the summer and not miss a word of their favorite soap opera because every radio would be tuned to it and in the days before air conditioning every window and many doors would be open.[218]

Stunts

• Of course, stunt men and stunt women played an important part in the filming of the 1960s tongue-in-cheek TV spy series *The Avengers*. However, you may be surprised to read that in some cases stunt men performed the stunts of Diana Rigg, who played Mrs. Emma Peel. For example, in the episode "The Bird Who Knew Too Much," Peter Elliott performs Mrs. Peel's high dive into the swimming pool. In many cases, however, stunt woman Cyd Child designed and performed Mrs. Peel's dangerous stunts.[219]

• In the TV series *The New Avengers*, actor Gareth Hunt performed a dangerous stunt in which he smashed through a glass window. In doing so, he cut his forehead and began bleeding. His co-star in the series, Patrick Macnee, who played an older John Steed, leaned down to him and said, "Dear boy, the biggest stunt I ever do is getting in and out of the car."[220]

Talk Shows

• An appearance on *The Tonight Show* with Johnny Carson could lead to fame and fortune and great success, and so of course many guests were understandably nervous before their first appearance on the TV program. The first time that movie critics Roger Ebert and Gene Siskel appeared on *The Tonight Show*, one of Johnny's writers stopped by their dressing room to say that Johnny would be asking them which current movies they liked. It's a good thing that the writer stopped by, for Mr. Ebert and Mr. Siskel were so nervous that they couldn't think of the titles of any current movies they liked, although several were playing that they had given thumbs-up to. With their minds completely blank, they brainstormed to come up with the title of a good movie. The only one they could think of was *Gone With the Wind*, so Mr. Siskel ended up calling their office back in Chicago and asking an assistant to tell them the titles of some movies they liked. (Of course, when they actually went on the show, Mr. Carson, always a master interviewer, put them at ease and everything went very smoothly.)[221]

• Before Mike Douglas' talk show was nationally syndicated, it was a locally produced show in Cleveland, Ohio. Once, Mr. Douglas decided to bring in a new, very talented singer named Barbra Streisand to appear on his show for a week. Unfortunately, he wasn't able to pay her enough money to live on. Therefore, he found her a singing job for a week in Cleveland, and she was able to make enough money to afford to appear on his talk show.[222]

• Comedian George Carlin once appeared on *The Tonight Show* with Johnny Carson and did an entire routine about the Vietnam War and other socially relevant issues. When he sat down, Mr. Carson said, "Wow! Pretty serious stuff." Mr. Carlin then explained that he could have spoken about innocuous stuff such as puppies and kittens, but since 5 million people were watching him, he had decided to say something important.[223]

• TV's Mister Rogers was Fred Rogers, who spoke in real life in the same slow way that he talked on the TV series. Once, Mister Rogers appeared on *The Tonight Show* with Johnny Carson, and Mr. Carson was so surprised that Mister Rogers spoke that way in real life that he found it difficult to keep from laughing. Mister Rogers told him, "You want to laugh, don't you? It's OK." And Johnny laughed.[224]

Telephones

• One of the most famous gimmicks in the 1960s TV series *Get Smart* is the shoe phone worn by Control agent Maxwell Smart. Years after *Get Smart* went off the air, Don Adams, the actor who played Maxwell Smart, would sometimes stop at a red light, and someone in the car next to his would roll down a window, hand him a shoe, and say, "It's for you."[225]

• As the wild-and-crazy character known as The Ghoul, Ron Sweed used to host mostly bad horror movies on a television station in

Cleveland, Ohio. The show's set included a telephone. Whenever The Ghoul had an incoming call, viewers at home heard the telephone emit a loud knock.[226]

Tobacco

• When TV was just becoming popular, cigarette companies sometimes sponsored shows and censored them. For example, when Camel, a cigarette brand, was the sponsor of a news program, it would not allow any "No Smoking" signs to be seen in the program's news footage, and it would not allow anyone to be seen smoking a cigar — with the exception of Winston Churchill, the Prime Minister of Great Britain.[227]

• W.C. Fields once was on a radio program sponsored by Lucky Strike cigarettes when he told a series of very funny stories about his nephew, Chester. The sponsors were not amused when they realized that Chester's full name — Chester Fields — was the name of a rival cigarette.[228]

Voices

• Ventriloquist Edgar Bergen and his partner, Charlie McCarthy (sometimes called a dummy, especially by W.C. Fields), wanted to be guests on the radio show starring Rudy Valle. However, an executive scoffed at the idea of a ventriloquist appearing on radio. During the audition, Mr. Bergen forgot his lines and asked for a look at the script. A young man showed Mr. Bergen the script, then started walking away. Suddenly, Charlie McCarthy's voice rang out: "Let me look at that." Without hesitation, the young man allowed Charlie McCarthy to "read" the script. The executive's jaw dropped, and he gave Mr. Bergen his start on radio.[229]

• Because the TV character Bart Simpson is a 10-year-old boy, people naturally expect a guy to provide his voice and not Nancy Cartwright, who does provide his voice, as well as the voices of Nelson and Ralph. One day, Ms. Cartwright was going shopping and did Bart's voice in the parking lot. A man heard her and said, "That's not Bart. I know the guy who does him." Ms. Cartwright said, "A guy does Bart's voice?" The man replied, "Yeah, that's right. Yours is pretty good, but it's not Bart."[230]

War

• War correspondent Christiane Amanpour got into broadcasting through an accident. One of her sisters paid tuition to attend a broadcasting school in London, then changed her mind. She asked for her tuition back, but it was not refundable. Therefore, Christiane asked if she could attend the school in her sister's place. This was acceptable, and she eventually became so famous that Pentagon officials once gave her an Amanpour Tracking Chart that detailed her journeys around the world to do reporting. Ms. Amanpour says, "They say I give great war. Is that sexual or what?"[231]

• When MacLean Stevenson, who played Colonel Blake, left the television sitcom *M*A*S*H*, his character's plane was shot down over the Sea of Japan — with no survivors. This was a bit of realism no TV sitcom had previously engaged in, and the episode's writers, Jim Fritzell and Everett Greenbaum, were both praised and d*mned by letter writers. To people who wrote him letters criticizing the decision to kill the character, Mr. Greenbaum wrote back, "The essence of war is the quick and final departure of a loved one."[232]

• As young soldiers during World War II, British comedian Spike Milligan and his friends took a dislike to a certain Bombardier while they were still stationed in England. They got their revenge when the Bombardier went to bed very drunk one night. They loaded him and his bed into a truck, then drove him to a cemetery, where they unloaded him and his bed, removed his pants, then drove back to the base. The Military Police found him the next day.[233]

• Back in the administration of George Bush, Sr., Defense Secretary Dick Cheney once flaunted a Bart Simpson doll dressed in camouflage. Matt Groening, the creator of *The Simpsons*, responded by saying, "It's always sad when a 10-year-old gets drawn into war."[234]

• Two days after Pearl Harbor, the radio show *Fibber McGee and Molly* made a joke about Japan. A character on the show said that he wanted to buy a globe, and Molly replied, "You want a globe with Japan on it? Then you better get one quick."[235]

• Norman Fell, who played Mr. Roper on the TV sitcom *Three's Company*, flew cargo planes during World War II. As he tells it, "I was getting shot at for 8,000 pounds of toilet paper."[236]

Work

• Tex Avery is the cartoonist who gave Bugs Buggy his distinctive personality. Before Mr. Avery started working on the Bugs Bunny cartoons, Bugs was a lot like Daffy Duck but in a rabbit suit. Mr. Avery gave Bugs a coolness and made him totally in control of every situation. The line "What's up, Doc?" actually came from the cool kids Mr. Avery remembered from his old high school in Dallas, Texas. Late in his career, when Mr. Avery was working on TV commercials, he directed a commercial featuring Bugs Bunny. Someone actually asked if he knew how to draw Bugs Bunny. About that experience, Mr. Avery says, "I think that's when I started making it clear just who created Bugs Bunny."[237]

• In one episode of *Mr. Ed* is a scene in which Wilbur, the character played by Alan Young, gave Mr. Ed a bath. After Mr. Ed had his bath, Wilbur was supposed to lose his balance and fall in the bath water. Unfortunately, during this scene, Mr. Ed had a bowel movement that fell in the tub. At this point, Mr. Young had to decide what to do. It was the end of the day (and the end of the week), the camera had not caught the bowel movement, and everyone — including himself and Mr. Ed — was tired. Stopping the scene would mean having to set up the scene again and reshoot it on Monday. All in all, a lot of work. So Mr. Young thought, "The h*ll with it," and Wilbur lost his balance and fell in the tub — then took a long, soapy shower.[238]

• Comedian Steve Allen once hosted a radio program on KNX, where his boss ordered him to "just play records, and in between do a little light chatter." Mr. Allen did that, but as time went on, the comedy took up more and more of the radio show, leaving little time for playing records. Therefore, his boss sent him a memo, telling him to stop the comedy and play the records. Mr. Allen read the memo on the air, then argued that anyone could play records but his comedy was original. Lots of listeners agreed with him, and 400 listeners sent in letters supporting him, so his boss told him to go ahead and do his comedy — "But play a little music, OK?"[239]

• As a young man, Matt Groening sent cartoons to his friends instead of letters. The cartoons documented his life in Los Angeles, and he titled the cartoons *Life in Hell*. They were good enough that he collected them in homemade comic books and sold them where he worked — a record store. Eventually, he hit what he calls the "doodlers' jackpot" of *The Simpsons* and *Futurama*. Meanwhile, all of his cartoonist friends who were more talented artists than he stopped creating and got boring, middle-class jobs.[240]

• Emma Caulfield played Anya the former vengeance demon on TV's *Buffy the Vampire Slayer*. Perhaps it is lucky that she got the job; after all, she admits to being a horrible waitress at a restaurant where she disliked the food. Customers would come in, ask what she recommended, and she would tell them that the food was very bad but the drinks were very good. Her customers ate little, but drank a lot and left her very generous, motivated-by-alcohol tips.[241]

• Comedian Henry Morgan once worked the late shift at a radio station. Among his other duties, he had to read a list of the people who were reported missing. Since he figured that at that late hour, no one was listening to the station, he included the name of his boss among the names of the people who had been reported missing. Mr. Morgan was wrong when he thought that no one was listening — his boss had been listening, so he was fired.[242]

• Robin Williams found out that his TV sitcom *Mork and Mindy* had been cancelled when he read about it in the trade newspapers —

the studio did not even show him the courtesy of calling him on the telephone first before releasing the news to the media. At the time, he was working with fellow comedian Eric Idle in *The Tale of the Frog Prince*, and he says, "I was so angry and hurt — and I was dressed as a frog!"[243]

• Before becoming famous on *Laugh-In*, comedian Lily Tomlin worked as a Howard Johnson's waitress. However, she got fired after grabbing the microphone and announcing, "Attention, diners. Your Howard Johnson's waitress of the week, Lily Tomlin, is about to make her appearance on the floor. Let's give her a big hand."[244]

• During the Joseph McCarthy hearings, TV viewers were fascinated. In fact, a TV was rented for employees at *The New Yorker* but returned after a few days — the staff tended to become so involved in watching the hearings that they forgot that they were supposed to be working on the next issue of the magazine.[245]

• Singer Al Jolson was a very popular guest star on radio programs — he once guested on 10 shows in one week! While he was guesting on the *Burns and Allen* program, Gracie asked why he didn't get his own program. Jolie replied, "What? And be on the radio only once a week?"[246]

Writers

• Monty Python member John Cleese once purchased a defective toaster, which made him very angry. He put his anger to use by writing a comedy sketch about his experience. Fellow Python member Graham Chapman often wrote with Mr. Cleese, and Mr. Cleese usually, but not always, ended up doing 80 percent of the work — sometimes he did 95 percent. Nevertheless, Mr. Chapman made some impressive contributions to the sketches. In this case, after Mr. Cleese had written a sketch about a defective toaster, Mr. Chapman said, "It's boring. Why not make it a parrot instead?" This suggestion resulted in one of Monty Python's most famous sketches — the Dead Parrot sketch, in which an irate man tries to return a dead parrot to a pet shop, whose owner insists that the parrot is only napping.[247]

• Some of the plots and dialogue on *The Dick Van Dyke Show* came from real life. The episode "A Bird in the Head Hurts!" was about a bird stalking Ritchie to get locks of his hair for her nest. (This actually happened to a neighbor of series creator Carl Reiner.) The advice given to Laura Petrie in the episode — "Let him wear a pith helmet" — was actually spoken by an ASPCA officer. In the episode "Never Name a Duck," the Petrie family acquires two ducks as pets for Ritchie. (In real life, the Reiner family had acquired two ducks as pets for the children.) One duck died and the other duck soon appeared to be ill. The line about the ill duck — "He looks pale!" — was spoken in real life by Mr. Reiner's wife, Estelle.[248]

• For a while, Marc Cherry, the openly gay creator of TV's *Desperate Housewives*, named every episode after a song title by Stephen Sondheim. This got Mr. Sondheim's attention, and Mr. Sondheim sent him this note: "Next time you're in town, give me a call and you can tell me how much you like my work." (Mr. Sondheim can get away with messages like that because he is so successful and because he is over 75 years old.) In fact, Mr. Cherry did get to have dinner with and spend five hours talking to Mr. Sondheim.[249]

• During the Joseph McCarthy era, and for a while after it, many excellent writers were blacklisted, meaning that they could not work in the entertainment industry. In practice, however, many of these writers continued to work, but their work appeared under the names of other people. For example, a blacklisted writer wrote an episode of *The Andy Griffith Show*, but the writer's name listed on the credits was chosen at random from the Los Angeles phone book.[250]

Appendix A: Bibliography

Adamson, Joe. *Tex Avery: King of Cartoons*. New York: Da Capo Press, Inc., 1985.

Adler, Bill. *Jewish Wit and Wisdom*. New York: Dell Publishing Co., Inc., 1969.

Adler, Bill. *The Letterman Wit: His Life and Humor*. New York: Carroll & Graf Publishers, Inc., 1994.

Allen, Steve. *More Funny People*. New York: Stein and Day, Publishers, 1982.

Anderson, Catherine Corley. *John F. Kennedy: Young People's President*. Minneapolis, MN: Lerner Publications Company, 1991.

Anderson, Marilyn D. *Sarah Michelle Gellar*. Philadelphia, PA: Chelsea House Publishers, 2002.

Arden, Eve. *Three Phases of Eve: An Autobiography*. New York: St. Martin's Press, 1985.

Berger, Phil. *The Last Laugh: The World of the Stand-Up Comics*. New York: William Morris and Co., Inc., 1975.

Billson, Anne. *Buffy the Vampire Slayer*. London: BFI Publishing, 1995.

Bono, Chastity. *Family Outing*. With Billie Fitzpatrick. Boston, MA: Little, Brown and Company, 1998.

Borge, Victor, and Robert Sherman. *My Favorite Comedies in Music*. New York: Franklin Watts, 1980.

Borns, Betsy. *Comic Lives: Inside the World of American Stand-Up Comedy*. New York: Simon and Schuster, Inc., 1987.

Brook, Donald. *Singers of Today*. Freeport, NY: Books for Libraries Press, 1971.

Bryan III, J. *Merry Gentlemen (and One Lady)*. New York: Atheneum, 1985.

Burns, George. *All My Best Friends*. Written with David Fisher. New York: Putnam Publishing Group, 1989.

Burns, George. *Gracie: A Love Story*. New York: G.P. Putnam's Sons, 1988.

Canemaker, John. *Tex Avery: The MGM Years, 1942-1955*. Atlanta, GA: Turner Publishing, Inc., 1996.

Carter, Judy. *Stand-Up Comedy: The Book*. New York: Dell Publishing, 1989.

Cartwright, Nancy. *My Life as a 10-Year-Old Boy*. New York: Hyperion, 2000.

Church, Carol Bauer. *Carol Burnett: Star of Comedy*. Minneapolis, MN: Greenhaven Press, Inc., 1976.

Claxton, William, photographer. *Laugh: Portraits of the Greatest Comedians and the Funny Stories They Tell Each Other*. Introduction by John Lithgow; conceived and produced by Andy Gould and Kathleen Bywater; text edited by Mike Thomas. New York: William Morrow, 1999.

Clinton, Kate. *Don't Get Me Started*. New York: Ballantine Books, 1998.

Cohen, Joel. *Odd Moments in Baseball.* New York: Scholastic, Inc., 2000.

Collier, Denise, and Kathleen Beckett. *Spare Ribs: Women in the Humor Biz.* New York: St. Martin's Press, 1980.

Crum, Jimmy, and Carole Gerber. *How About That! Jimmy Crum: Fifty Years of Cliffhangers and Barn-Burners.* Columbus, OH: Fine Line Graphics, 1993.

Cruz, Barbara C. Ru*bén Blades: Salsa Singer and Social Activist.* Springfield, NJ: Enslow Publications, Inc., 1997.

Damon, Duane. *Headin' for Better Times.* Minneapolis, MN: Lerner Publications Company, 2002.

Day, Nancy. *Advertising: Information or Manipulation?* Springfield, NJ: Enslow Publications, Inc., 1999.

Denver, Bob. *Gilligan, Maynard and Me.* New York: Carol Publishing Group, 1993.

Diller, Phyllis. *Like a Lampshade in a Whorehouse: My Life in Comedy.* With Richard Buskin. London: Penguin Group, 2005.

Doner, W.B., and Company. *Likeable Advertising.* Southfield, MI: W.B. Doner and Company, 1988.

Donnelly, Liza. *Funny Ladies: The New Yorker's Greatest Women Cartoonists and Their Cartoons.* Amherst, NY: Prometheus Books, 2005.

Doonan, Simon. *Confessions of a Window Dresser.* New York: Penguin Studio, 1998.

Drucker, Hal, and Sid Lerner. *From the Desk Of.* Photographs by Sing-Si Schwartz. San Diego, CA: Harcourt Brace Jovanovich, Publishers, 1989.

Epstein, Lawrence J. *Mixed Nuts: America's Love Affair with Comedy Teams From Burns and Allen to Belushi and Aykroyd.* New York: PublicAffairs, 2004.

Erskine, Carl. *Carl Erskine's Tales from the Dodger Dugout.* Champaigne, IL: Sports Publishing, Inc., 2000.

Feran, Tom, and R.D. Heldenfels. *Ghoulardi: Inside Cleveland TV's Wildest Ride.* Cleveland, OH: Gray & Company, Publishers, 1997.

Fletcher, Lynne Yamaguchi. *The First Gay Pope and Other Records.* Boston, MA: Alyson Publications, Inc., 1992.

Franklin, Joe. *Joe Franklin's Encyclopedia of Comedians.* Secaucus, NJ: The Citadel Press, 1979.

Freberg, Stan. *It Only Hurts When I Laugh.* New York: Times Books, 1988.

Funny Gay Males (a comedy troupe consisting of Jaffe Cohen, Danny McWilliams, and Bob Smith). *Growing Up Gay.* New York: Hyperion, 1995.

Garner, Joe. *Made You Laugh: the Funniest Moments in Radio, Television, Stand-up, and Movie Comedy.* Kansas City, MO: Andrews McMeel Publishing, 2004.

Garner, Joe. *Stay Tuned: Television's Unforgettable Moments*. Kansas City, MO: Andrews McMeel Publishing, 2002.

Gonzales, Doreen. *Madeleine L'Engle, Author of* A Wrinkle in Time. New York: Dillon Press, 1991.

Green, Joey. *The Get Smart Handbook*. New York: Collier Books, 1993.

Green, Joey. *Hi Bob! The Unofficial Guide to The Bob Newhart Show*. New York: St. Martin's Griffin, 1996. Advance uncorrected proofs.

Greenberg, Keith Elliot. *Charles, Burrows, and Charles: TV's Top Producers*. Woodbridge, CT: Blackbirch Press, Inc., 1995.

Hanff, Helene. *Apple of My Eye*. Wakefield, RI: Moyer Bell, 1988.

Harmon, Jim. *The Great Radio Comedians*. Garden City, NY: Doubleday and Company, Inc., 1970.

Harmon, Jim. *The Great Radio Heroes*. Jefferson, NC, and London: McFarland and Company, Inc., Publishers, 2001.

Havens, Candace. *Joss Whedon: The Genius Behind Buffy*. Dallas, TX: BenBella Books, 2003.

Hay, Peter. *Canned Laughter*. New York: Oxford University Press, 1992.

Hecht, Andrew. *Hollywood Merry-Go-Round*. New York: Grosset and Dunlap, Publishers, 1947.

Hollingsworth, Amy. *The Simple Faith of Mister Rogers*. Nashville, TN: Integrity Publishers, 2005.

Horowitz, Susan. *Queens of Comedy*. Australia: Gordon and Breach, Publishers, 1997.

Javna, John. *The Best of TV Sitcoms*. New York: Harmony Books, 1988.

Jewell, Geri. *Geri*. With Stewart Weiner. New York: William Morrow and Co., Inc., 1984.

Johnson, Russell, and Steve Cox. *Here on Gilligan's Isle*. New York: HarperCollins Publishers, Inc., 1993.

Kanner, Bernice. *The 100 Best TV Commercials ... and Why They Worked*. New York: Times Books, 1999.

Katkov, Norman. *The Fabulous Fanny*. New York: Alfred A. Knopf, 1953.

Kelly, Richard. *The Andy Griffith Show*. Winston-Salem, NC: John F. Blair, Publisher, 1981.

Kent, Allegra. *Once a Dancer ...*. New York: St. Martin's Press, 1997.

Keyes, Daniel. Algernon, *Charlie and I: A Writer's Journey*. Boca Raton, FL: Challcrest Press Books, 1999.

Knotts, Don. *Barney Fife and Other Characters I Have Known*. With Robert Metz. New York: Berkley Boulevard Books, 1999.

Leno, Jay. *Leading With My Chin*. With Bill Zehme. New York: HarperCollins Publishers, Inc., 1996.

Leonard, Sheldon. *And the Show Goes On: Broadway and Hollywood Adventures*. New York: Limelight, 1994.

Linkletter, Art. Kids Say the Darndest Things! New York: Bonanza Books, 1978.

Linkletter, Art. *Oops! Or, Life's Awful Moments*. Garden City, NY: Doubleday & Company, Inc., 1967.

Macnee, Patrick. *The Avengers and Me*. With Dave Rogers. New York: TV Books, 1997.

Macnee, Patrick, and Marie Cameron. *Blind in One Ear: The Avenger Returns*. San Francisco, CA: Mercury House, Inc., 1989.

Malloy, Merrit, and Marsha Rose. *Comedians' Quote Book*. New York: Sterling Publishing Co., Inc, 1993.

Mander, Jerry. *Four Arguments for the Elimination of Television*. New York: William Morrow and Company, Inc., 1978.

Mason, Paul. *Sarah Michelle Gellar*. Chicago, IL: Raintree, 2005.

Meadows, Audrey. *Love, Alice: My Life as a Honeymooner*. With Joe Daley. New York: Crown Publishers, Inc., 1994.

Miller, John and Kirsten. *Legends 2: Women Who Have*

Changed the World, Through the Eyes of Great Women Writers. Novato, CA: New World Library, 2004.

Miller, Toby. *The Avengers*. London: British Film Institute, 1997.

Milligan, Spike. *Adolf Hitler: My Part in His Downfall*. London: Michael Joseph, Limited, 1971.

Mingo, Jack, and Erin Barrett. *Lunchbox: From Comic Books to Cult TV and Beyond*. New York: HarperEntertainment, 2004.

Moore, Mary Tyler. *After All*. New York: G.P. Putnam's Sons, 1995.

Moore, Michael. *Stupid White Men*. New York: HarperCollins Publishers, Inc., 2001.

Morgan, David. *Monty Python Speaks*. New York: Avon Books, Inc., 1999.

Morgan, Henry. *Here's Morgan!* New York: Barricade Books, Inc., 1994.

Morella, Joe, and Edward Z. Epstein. *Forever Lucy*. New York: Berkley Books, 1990.

Morley, Robert. *Robert Morley's Book of Bricks*. New York: G.P. Putnam's Sons, 1979.

Morton, Robert, editor. *Stand-up Comedians on Television*. New York: Harry N. Abrams, Inc. [in association with] The Museum of Television & Radio, 1996.

Mott, Robert L. *Radio Live! Television Live!: Those Golden Days When Horses Were Coconuts*. Jefferson, NC: McFarland & Company, Inc., Publishers, 2000.

Music Educators National Conference, editors. *The Gifts of Music*. Reston, VA: Music Educators National Conference, 1994.

Nachman, Gerald. *Seriously Funny: The Rebel Comedians of the 1950s and 1960s*. New York: Pantheon Books, 2003.

Nash, Bruce, and Allan Zullo. *The Hollywood Walk of Shame*. Compiled by Martha Moffett. Kansas City, MO: Andrews and McMeel, 1993.

Neuwirth, Allan. *They'll Never Put That on the Air: An Oral History of Taboo-Breaking TV Comedy*. New York: Allworth Press, 2006.

Newman, Matthew. *Brandy*. Philadelphia, PA: Chelsea House Publishers, 2001.

O'Connell, Charles. *The Other Side of the Record*. New York: Alfred A. Knopf, 1949.

Orleans, Ellen. *Can't Keep a Straight Face*. Bala Cynwyd, PA: Laugh Lines Press, 1992.

Paulsen, Gary. *How Angel Peterson Got His Name and Other Outrageous Tales About Extreme Sports*. New York: Wendy Lamb Books, 2003.

Pegg, Robert. *Comical Co-Stars of Television*. Jefferson, NC: McFarland & Company, Inc., Publishers, 2002.

Price, Vincent. *The Book of Joe*. Garden City, NY: Doubleday & Co., Inc., 1961.

Riley, Gail Blasser. *Wah Ming Chang: Artist and Master of Special Effects*. Springfield, NJ: Enslow Publications, Inc., 1995.

Ritts, Paul. *The TV Jeebies*. Philadelphia, PA: The John C. Winston Company, 1951.

Robinson, Simon. *A Year With Rudolf Nureyev*. With Derek Robinson. London: Robert Hale, Limited, 1997.

Rogers, Dave. *The Avengers*. London: Independent Television Books, Ltd., 1983.

Rogers, Dave. *The Avengers Anew*. London: Michael Joseph, Ltd., 1985.

Rogers, Fred. *You Are Special*. New York: Viking, 1994.

Rozakis, Laurie. *Hanna and Barbera: Yabba-Dabba-Doo!* Woodbridge, CT: Blackbirch Press, Inc., 1994.

Rubin, Stephen E. *The New Met in Profile*. New York: Macmillan Publishing Co., Inc., 1974.

Saidman, Anne. *Oprah Winfrey: Media Success Story*. Minneapolis, MN: Lerner Publications Company, 1990.

Sanford, Herb. *Ladies and Gentlemen, The Garry Moore Show: Behind the Scenes When TV was New*. New York: Stein and Day, Publishers, 1976.

Schafer, Kermit. *All Time Great Bloopers*. New York: Avenel Books, 1973.

Schafer, Kermit. *Best of Bloopers*. New York: Avenel Books, 1973.

Schuman, Michael A. *Will Smith: "I Like Blending a Message with Comedy."* Berkeley Heights, NJ: Enslow Publishers, Inc., 2006.

Scott, Kieran. *James Van Der Beek*. New York: Aladdin Paperbacks, 1999.

Silverman, Stephen M. *Funny Ladies: The Women Who Make Us Laugh*. New York: Harry N. Abrams, Inc., 1999.

Smith, H. Allen. *Lost in the Horse Latitudes*. Garden City, NY: Doubleday, Doran, and Co., 1944.

Smith, Ron. *Comic Support*. New York: Carol Publishing Group, 1993.

Sorensen, Jeff. *Lily Tomlin: Woman of a Thousand Faces*. New York: St. Martin's Press, 1989.

Stafford, Nikki, editor. *Trekkers: True Stories by Fans for Fans*. Toronto, Ontario, Canada: ECW Press, 2002.

Steffens, Bradley, and Robyn M. Weaver. *Cartoonists*. San Diego, CA: Lucent Books, 2000.

Stefoff, Rebecca. *Mary Tyler Moore: The Woman Behind the Smile*. New York: New American Library, 1986.

Stine, R.L. *It Came From Ohio: My Life as a Writer*. As told to Joe Arthur. New York: Scholastic, Inc., 1997.

Stone, Laurie. *Laughing in the Dark: A Decade of Subversive Comedy*. Hopewell, NJ: The Ecco Press, 1997.

Sweed, Ron "The Ghoul," and Mike Olszewski. *The Ghoul Scrapbook*. Cleveland, OH: Gray and Company, Publishers, 1998.

Taylor, Glenhall. *Before Television: The Radio Years*. New York: A.S. Barnes and Company, 1979.

Terry-Thomas, and Terry Daum. *Terry-Thomas ... Tells Tales*. London: Robson Books, 1990.

Took, Barry. *Comedy Greats: A Celebration of Comic Genius Past and Present*. Wellingborough, Northamptonshire, England: Equation, 1989.

Tracy, Kathleen. *The Girl's Got Bite*. New York: St. Martin's Press, 2003.

Ullman, Tracey. *Tracey Takes On*. New York: Hyperion, 1998.

Unterbrink, Mary. *Funny Women: American Comediennes, 1860-1985*. Jefferson, NC: McFarland and Co., Inc., Publishers, 1987.

Vilanch, Bruce. *Bruce! Adventures in the Skin Trade and Other Essays*. New York: Jeremy P. Tarcher/Putnam, 2000.

Waldron, Vince. *Classic Sitcoms: A Celebration of the Best in Prime-Time Comedy*. New York: Macmillan Publishing Company, 1987.

Waters, John. *Crackpot: The Obsessions of John Waters*. New York: Vintage Books, 1987.

Weissman, Ginny, and Coyne Steven Sanders. *The Dick Van Dyke Show*. New York: St. Martin's Press, 1993.

Welles, Orson, and Peter Bogdanovich. *This is Orson Welles*. Edited by Jonathan Rosenbaum. New York: HarperCollins Publishers, 1992.

White, Betty. *Here We Go Again: My Life in Television*. New York: St. Martin's Press, 1995.

Wooten, Sara McIntosh. *Oprah Winfrey: Talk Show Legend*. Berkeley Heights, NJ: Enslow Publications, Inc., 1999.

Young, Alan, and Bill Burt. *Mr. Ed and Me*. New York: St. Martin's Press, 1994.

Appendix B: About the Author

It was a dark and stormy night. Suddenly a cry rang out, and on a hot summer night in 1954, Josephine, wife of Carl Bruce, gave birth to a boy — me. Unfortunately, this young married couple allowed Reuben Saturday, Josephine's brother, to name their first-born. Reuben, aka "The Joker," decided that Bruce was a nice name, so he decided to name me Bruce Bruce. I have gone by my middle name — David — ever since.

Being named Bruce David Bruce hasn't been all bad. Bank tellers remember me very quickly, so I don't often have to show an ID. It can be fun in charades, also. When I was a counselor as a teenager at Camp Echoing Hills in Warsaw, Ohio, a fellow counselor gave the signs for "sounds like" and "two words," then she pointed to a bruise on her leg twice. Bruise Bruise? Oh yeah, Bruce Bruce is the answer!

Uncle Reuben, by the way, gave me a haircut when I was in kindergarten. He cut my hair short and shaved a small bald spot on the back of my head. My mother wouldn't let me go to school until the bald spot grew out again.

Of all my brothers and sisters (six in all), I am the only transplant to Athens, Ohio. I was born in Newark, Ohio, and have lived all around Southeastern Ohio. However, I moved to Athens to go to Ohio University and have never left.

At Ohio U, I never could make up my mind whether to major in English or Philosophy, so I got a bachelor's degree with a double major in both areas, then I added a Master of Arts degree in English and a Master of Arts degree in Philosophy. Yes, I have my MAMA degree.

Currently, and for a long time to come (I eat fruits and veggies), I am spending my retirement writing books such as *Nadia Comaneci: Perfect 10*, *The Funniest People in Comedy*, *Homer's* Iliad: *A Retelling in Prose*, and *William Shakespeare's* Hamlet: *A Retelling in Prose.*

If all goes well, I will publish one or two books a year for the rest of my life. (On the other hand, a good way to make God laugh is to tell Her your plans.)

By the way, my sister Brenda Kennedy writes romances such as *A New Beginning* and *Shattered Dreams.*

Appendix C: Some Books by David Bruce

Anecdote Collections

250 Anecdotes About Opera
250 Anecdotes About Religion
250 Anecdotes About Religion: Volume 2
250 Music Anecdotes
Be a Work of Art: 250 Anecdotes and Stories
The Coolest People in Art: 250 Anecdotes
The Coolest People in the Arts: 250 Anecdotes
The Coolest People in Books: 250 Anecdotes
The Coolest People in Comedy: 250 Anecdotes
Create, Then Take a Break: 250 Anecdotes
Don't Fear the Reaper: 250 Anecdotes
The Funniest People in Art: 250 Anecdotes
The Funniest People in Books: 250 Anecdotes
The Funniest People in Books, Volume 2: 250 Anecdotes
The Funniest People in Books, Volume 3: 250 Anecdotes
The Funniest People in Comedy: 250 Anecdotes
The Funniest People in Dance: 250 Anecdotes
The Funniest People in Families: 250 Anecdotes
The Funniest People in Families, Volume 2: 250 Anecdotes
The Funniest People in Families, Volume 3: 250 Anecdotes
The Funniest People in Families, Volume 4: 250 Anecdotes
The Funniest People in Families, Volume 5: 250 Anecdotes
The Funniest People in Families, Volume 6: 250 Anecdotes
The Funniest People in Movies: 250 Anecdotes
The Funniest People in Music: 250 Anecdotes
The Funniest People in Music, Volume 2: 250 Anecdotes
The Funniest People in Music, Volume 3: 250 Anecdotes
The Funniest People in Neighborhoods: 250 Anecdotes
The Funniest People in Relationships: 250 Anecdotes
The Funniest People in Sports: 250 Anecdotes
The Funniest People in Sports, Volume 2: 250 Anecdotes
The Funniest People in Television and Radio: 250 Anecdotes
The Funniest People in Theater: 250 Anecdotes

The Funniest People Who Live Life: 250 Anecdotes
The Funniest People Who Live Life, Volume 2: 250 Anecdotes
The Kindest People Who Do Good Deeds, Volume 1: 250 Anecdotes
The Kindest People Who Do Good Deeds, Volume 2: 250 Anecdotes
Maximum Cool: 250 Anecdotes
The Most Interesting People in Movies: 250 Anecdotes
The Most Interesting People in Politics and History: 250 Anecdotes
The Most Interesting People in Politics and History, Volume 2: 250 Anecdotes
The Most Interesting People in Politics and History, Volume 3: 250 Anecdotes
The Most Interesting People in Religion: 250 Anecdotes
The Most Interesting People in Sports: 250 Anecdotes
The Most Interesting People Who Live Life: 250 Anecdotes
The Most Interesting People Who Live Life, Volume 2: 250 Anecdotes
Reality is Fabulous: 250 Anecdotes and Stories
Resist Psychic Death: 250 Anecdotes
Seize the Day: 250 Anecdotes and Stories

[1] Source: Nikki Stafford, editor, *Trekkers: True Stories by Fans for Fans*, pp. 153-154.

[2] Source: Josh Whedon Interview, "Passion," *Buffy the Vampire Slayer*: The Complete Second Season on DVD.

[3] Source: Joey Green, *Hi Bob!*, pp. 184, 186.

[4] Source: Barbara C. Cruz, *Rubén Blades: Salsa Singer and Social Activist*, p. 79.

[5] Source: Glenhall Taylor, *Before Television*, pp. 67-68.

[6] Source: Joe Franklin, *Joe Franklin's Encyclopedia of Comedians*, p. 134.

[7] Source: Joey Green, *The Get Smart Handbook*, p. 237.

[8] Source: Patrick Macnee, *The Avengers and Me*, pp. 48-49.

[9] Source: Marilyn D. Anderson, *Sarah Michelle Gellar*, p. 36.

[10] Source: Jim Harmon, *The Great Radio Heroes*, pp. 191-192.

[11] Source: Jack Mingo and Erin Barrett, *Lunchbox*, p. 63.

[12] Source: Phyllis Diller, *Like a Lampshade in a Whorehouse: My Life in Comedy*, pp. 191-192.

[13] Source: Alan Young, *Mr. Ed and Me*, p. 10.

[14] Source: Mary Unterbrink, *Funny Women*, p. 144.

[15] Source: Geri Jewell, *Geri*, pp. 247-248.

[16] Source: George Burns, *All My Best Friends*, p. 266.

[17] Source: W.B. Doner and Company, *Likeable Advertising*, pp. 14-15.

[18] Source: Jimmy Crum and Carole Gerber, *How About That!*, p. 16.

[19] Source: Allegra Kent, *Once a Dancer...*, p. 240.

[20] Source: Peter Hay, *Canned Laughter*, p. 208.

[21] Source: Bernice Kanner, *The 100 Best TV Commercials*, p. 176.

[22] Source: Barry Took, *Comedy Greats*, p. 199.

[23] Source: Jim Harmon, *The Great Radio Heroes*, p. 110.

[24] Source: Robert Morton, editor, *Stand-up Comedians on Television*, p. 111.

[25] Source: Robert Pegg, *Comical Co-Stars of Television*, p. 110.

[26] Source: Nancy Day, *Advertising: Information or Manipulation?*, p. 59.

[27] Source: John Javna, *The Best of TV Sitcoms*, p. 12.

[28] Source: George Burns, *Gracie: A Love Story*, pp. 100ff.

[29] Source: Jeff Sorensen, *Lily Tomlin: Woman of a Thousand Faces*, p. 45.

[30] Source: Carl Erskine, *Carl Erskine's Tales from the Dodger Dugout*, pp. 5-6.

[31] Source: Keith Elliot Greenberg, *Charles, Burrows, and Charles: TV's Top Producers*, pp. 64-65.

[32] Source: David Morgan, *Monty Python Speaks*, p. 90.

[33] Source: Andrew Hecht, *Hollywood Merry-Go-Round*, p. 186.

[34] Source: Merrit Malloy and Marsha Rose, *Comedians' Quote Book*, p. 74.

[35] Source: Terry-Thomas, *Terry-Thomas Tells Tales*, p. 125.

[36] Source: Betty White, *Here We Go Again*, pp. xv, 15.

[37] Source: Vincent Price, *The Book of Joe*, pp. 98-99.

[38] Source: Stephen E. Rubin, *The New Met in Profile*, p. 38.

[39] Source: SUNY-95, a Columbus, Ohio, radio station. Also: A Channel 4 newscast in Columbus, Ohio.

[40] Source: Patrick Macnee and Marie Cameron, *Blind in One Ear*, pp. 152, 154.

[41] Source: Phil Berger, *The Last Laugh*, p. 50.

[42] Source: Spike Milligan, *Adolf Hitler: My Part in His Downfall*, p. 138.

[43] Source: Simon Robinson, *A Year With Rudolf Nureyev*, pp. 142-143.

[44] Source: Stan Freberg, *It Only Hurts When I Laugh*, p. 90.

[45] Source: Paul Ritts, *The TV Jeebies*, pp. 124-126.

[46] Source: Matthew Newman, *Brandy*, pp. 16, 21-22.

[47] Source: Laura Barton, "I make lemons into lemonade." *The Guardian*. 1 September 2006 <www.guardian.co.uk/g2/story/0,,1862467,00.html>.

[48] Source: Susan Horowitz, *Queens of Comedy*, p. 22.

[49] Source: Toby Miller, *The Avengers*, pp. 148-149.

[50] Source: Bruce Nash and Allan Zullo, *The Hollywood Walk of Shame*, p. 74.

[51] Source: Helene Hanff, *Apple of My Eye*, p. vii.

[52] Source: Robert L. Mott, *Radio Live! Television Live!*, pp. 79-81.

[53] Source: Tracey Ullman, *Tracey Takes On*, p. 141.

[54] Source: Russell Johnson and Steve Cox, *Here on Gilligan's Isle*, p. 28.

[55] Source: Laurie Rozakis, *Hanna and Barbera: Yabba-Dabba-Doo!*, pp. 20, 29-30.

[56] Source: Joe Adamson, *Tex Avery: King of Cartoons*, p. 167.

[57] Source: Gerald Nachman, *Seriously Funny*, p. 458.

[58] Source: Robert L. Mott, *Radio Live! Television Live!*, p. 5.

[59] Source: Hadley Freeman, "A walking soap opera." *The Guardian*. 11 June 2007 <http://www.guardian.co.uk/g2/story/0,,2099932,00.html>.

[60] Source: Joe Morella and Edward Z. Epstein, *Forever Lucy*, p. 10.

[61] Source: Gary Paulsen, *How Angel Peterson Got His Name and Other Outrageous Tales About Extreme Sports*, pp. 4-5.

[62] Source: Art Linkletter, *Kids Say the Darndest Things!*, p. 18.

[63] Source: R.L. Stine, *It Came From Ohio: My Life as a Writer*, p. 104.

[64] Source: Geri Jewell, *Geri*, p. 116.

[65] Source: Doreen Gonzales, *Madeleine L'Engle, Author of* A Wrinkle in Time, pp. 76, 91.

[66] Source: Carol Bauer Church, *Carol Burnett: Star of Comedy*, p. 7.

[67] Source: Joe Adamson, *Tex Avery: King of Cartoons*, pp. 133-134.

[68] Source: Amy Hollingsworth, *The Simple Faith of Mister Rogers*, p. 156.

[69] Source: Bob Denver, *Gilligan, Maynard and Me*, p. 174.

[70] Source: Eve Arden, *Three Phases of Eve*, p. 73.

[71] Source: Patrick Macnee and Marie Cameron, *Blind in One Ear*, p. 34.

[72] Source: Nancy Cartwright, *My Life as a 10-Year-Old Boy*, p. 172.

[73] Source: Art Linkletter, *Kids Say the Darndest Things!*, p. 95.

[74] Source: Fred Rogers, *You Are Special*, p. 34.

[75] Source: Betsy Borns, *Comic Lives*, pp. 97-98.

[76] Source: Denise Collier and Kathleen Beckett, *Spare Ribs*, p. 80.

[77] Source: Music Educators National Conference, editors, *The Gifts of Music*, p. 138.

[78] Source: Susan Horowitz, *Queens of Comedy*, p. 70.

[79] Source: Bob Denver, *Gilligan, Maynard and Me*, p. 135.

[80] Source: Laurie Stone, *Laughing in the Dark*, p. 160.

[81] Source: Dave Rogers, *The Avengers*, p. 31.

[82] Source: Mary Unterbrink, *Funny Women*, p. 69.

[83] Source: Richard Kelly, *The Andy Griffith Show*, p. 137.

[84] Source: Don Knotts, *Barney Fife and Other Characters I Have Known*, p. 128.

[85] Source: Joe Garner, *Stay Tuned: Television's Unforgettable Moments*, pp. 13-14.

[86] Source: Joe Garner, *Made You Laugh*, pp. 88-90.

[87] Source: Herb Sanford, *Ladies and Gentlemen, The Garry Moore Show: Behind the Scenes When TV was New*, p. 153.

[88] Source: George Burns, *All My Best Friends*, p. 283.

[89] Source: Judy Carter, *Stand-Up Comedy: The Book*, p. 12.

[90] Source: Anne Billson, *Buffy the Vampire Slayer*, pp. 101, 104, 120, 130. Also, a documentary included in the *Buffy* Season 6 DVD collection (Disk 3 Special Feature: a 2002 Academy of Television Arts and Sciences Panel Discussion) and an article on "Shut Up, Dawn" at <http://uncoolkids.com/buffy/?p=21>.

[91] Source: Steve Allen, *More Funny People*, p. 38.

[92] Source: Jerry Mander, *Four Arguments for the Elimination of Television*, p. 341.

[93] Source: J. Bryan III, *Merry Gentlemen (and One Lady)*, p. 77.

[94] Source: Candace Havens, *Joss Whedon: The Genius Behind Buffy*, pp. 76-77.

[95] Source: Jay Leno, *Leading With My Chin*, pp. 48-49.

[96] Source: Norman Katkov, *Fabulous Fanny*, pp. 304, 307.

[97] Source: Ron Smith, *Comic Support*, p. 204.

[98] Source: Music Educators National Conference, editors, *The Gifts of Music*, p. 47.

[99] Source: Michael Moore, *Stupid White Men*, p. 91.

[100] Source: "Foreword," by Sherwood Schwartz, in Russell Johnson and Steve Cox's *Here on Gilligan's Isle*, pp. xi-xii.

[101] Source: Kathleen Tracy, *The Girl's Got Bite*, p. 89.

[102] Source: Anne Saidman, *Oprah Winfrey: Media Success Story*, pp. 7-8.

[103] Source: Andrew Hecht, *Hollywood Merry-Go-Round*, p. 179.

[104] Source: Laura Barton, "I make lemons into lemonade." *The Guardian*. 1 September 2006 <http://www.guardian.co.uk/g2/story/0,,1862467,00.html>.

[105] Source: George Burns, *Gracie: A Love Story*, p. 178.

[106] Source: Steve Allen, *More Funny People*, pp. 241-242.

[107] Source: Michael Jensen, "Interview with Michael Urie." 31 October 2007 <http://www.afterelton.com/people/2007/11/michael_urie>.

[108] Source: Stan Freberg, *It Only Hurts When I Laugh*, p. 73.

[109] Source: Anne Billson, *Buffy the Vampire Slayer*, p. 6.

[110] Source: John Waters, *Crackpot: The Obsessions of John Waters*, p. 66.

[111] Source: Funny Gay Males, *Growing Up Gay*, p. 144.

[112] Source: Betsy Borns, *Comic Lives*, p. 26.

[113] Source: Robert Pegg, *Comical Co-Stars of Television*, p, 90.

[114] Source: Ginny Weissman and Coyne Steven Sanders, *The Dick Van Dyke Show*, p. 2.

[115] Source: Orson Welles and Peter Bogdanovich, *This is Orson Welles*, p. xxii.

[116] Source: Allegra Kent, *Once a Dancer...*, p. 255.

[117] Source: Joe Franklin, *Joe Franklin's Encyclopedia of Comedians*, p. 36.

[118] Source: Mary Tyler Moore, *After All*, pp. 110-111.

[119] Source: R.L. Stine, *It Came From Ohio: My Life as a Writer*, p. 122.

[120] Source: Joe Morella and Edward Z. Epstein, *Forever Lucy*, p. 19.

[121] Source: Denise Collier and Kathleen Beckett, *Spare Ribs*, p. 179.

[122] Source: Brenda Scott Royce, *Hogan's Heroes*, p. 10.

[123] Source: Christie Keith, "Xena and Gabrielle Still Going Strong." 21 January 2007 <http://www.afterellen.com/node/4575>.

[124] Source: Shauna Swartz, "Air America's lesbian host on growing up, coming out, and turning on to radio." 29 January 2007 <http://www.afterellen.com/node/4736>.

[125] Source: Neal Broverman, "Glass on glass." *The Advocate*. 9 April 2007 <http://www.advocate.com/exclusive_detail_ektid44218.asp>.

[126] Source: Cornelius Delro, "Black Comedians Perpetuate, Challenge Gay Stereotypes." 12 May 2007 <http://www.afterelton.com/people/2005/5/comedians.html>.

[127] Source: Bruce Vilanch, *Bruce! Adventures in the Skin Trade and Other Essays*, pp. 9-10. Also: *The Hollywood Squares.*

[128] Source: Chastity Bono, *Family Outing*, p. 77.

[129] Source: Funny Gay Males, *Growing Up Gay*, p. 131.

[130] Source: Lynne Yamaguchi Fletcher, *The First Gay Pope and Other Records*, p. 118.

[131] Source: Robert Urban, "The Men of Sirius OutQ Radio: Jeremy Hovies." 17 May 2005 <http://www.afterelton.com/music/2005/5/sirius-hovies.html>.

[132] Source: Simon Doonan, *Confessions of a Window Dresser*, p. 45.

[133] Source: Chastity Bono, *Family Outing*, p. 31.

[134] Source: Ellen Orleans, *Can't Keep a Straight Face*, pp. 71-72.

[135] Source: Catherine Corley Anderson, *John F. Kennedy: Young People's President*, pp. 57-59.

[136] Source: Sara McIntosh Wooten, *Oprah Winfrey: Talk Show Legend*, p. 83.

[137] Source: Robert Morton, editor, *Stand-up Comedians on Television*, p. 88.

[138] Source: Bill Adler, *The Letterman Wit: His Life and Humor*, p. 33.

[139] Source: William Claxton, *Laugh*, p. 62.

[140] Source: Bernice Kanner, *The 100 Best TV Commercials*, p. 225.

[141] Source: Kermit Schafer, *Best of Bloopers*, p. 78.

[142] Source: Roger Ebert, "Answer Man." 18 September 2005 <http://rogerebert.suntimes.com/apps/pbcs.dll/section?category=ANSWERMAN>.

[143] Source: Eve Arden, *Three Phases of Eve*, p. 183.

[144] Source: Brenda Scott Royce, *Hogan's Heroes*, p. 134.

[145] Source: Bruce Vilanch, *Bruce! Adventures in the Skin Trade and Other Essays*, pp. 19-20.

[146] Source: Dave Rogers, *The Avengers Anew*, p. 85.

[147] Source: Henry Morgan, *Here's Morgan!*, p. 109.

[148] Source: Paul Mason, *Sarah Michelle Gellar*, pp. 9, 11.

[149] Source: Joel Cohen, *Odd Moments in Baseball*, p. 95.

[150] Source: Bruce Nash and Allan Zullo, *The Hollywood Walk of Shame*, p. 43.

[151] Source: Daniel Keyes, *Algernon, Charlie and I: A Writer's Journey*, p. 132.

[152] Source: Carl Erskine, *Carl Erskine's Tales from the Dodger Dugout*, p. 9.

[153] Source: Audrey Meadows, *Love, Alice*, pp. 175-176.

[154] Source: Joey Green, *Hi Bob!*, p. 3.

[155] Source: Allan Neuwirth, *They'll Never Put That on the Air*, pp. 32-33.

[156] Source: Paul Ritts, *The TV Jeebies*, pp. 32-34, 37-38, 42.

[157] Source: Kieran Scott, *James Van Der Beek*, pp. 9-10, 12, 20.

[158] Source: William Claxton, *Laugh*, p. 55.

[159] Source: W.B. Doner and Company, *Likeable Advertising*, pp. 8-9.

[160] Source: Glenhall Taylor, *Before Television*, p. 87.

[161] Source: Art Linkletter, *Oops!*, pp. 44-45.

[162] Source: Charles O'Connell, *The Other Side of the Record*, p. 24.

[163] Source: Lawrence J. Epstein, *Mixed Nuts*, p. 53.

[164] Source: Brian Rose, an archeologist.

[165] Source: Robert Morley, *Robert Morley's Book of Bricks*, p. 148.

[166] Source: Anne Saidman, *Oprah Winfrey: Media Success Story*, p. 20.

[167] Source: Kermit Schafer, *All Time Great Bloopers*, p. 21.

[168] Source: Rebecca Stefoff, *Mary Tyler Moore: The Woman Behind the Smile*, pp. 57-58.

[169] Source: Bradley Steffens and Robyn M. Weaver, *Cartoonists*, p. 76.

[170] Source: Tracey Ullman, *Tracey Takes On*, p. xi.

[171] Source: Jeffrey Epstein, "Kristen Bell." 14 May 2006 <http://www.out.com/detail.asp?id=17416>.

[172] Source: Kermit Schafer, *All Time Great Bloopers*, p. 29.

[173] Source: Hal Drucker and Sid Lerner, *From the Desk Of*, p. 14.

[174] Source: Bill Adler, *Jewish Wit and Wisdom*, pp. 78-79.

[175] Source: Ken Levine, "19-cent cheques leave writers wanting change." *Toronto Star*. 4 November 2007 <http://www.thestar.com/entertainment/article/273331>.

[176] Source: Donald Brook, *Singers of Today*, p. 218.

[177] Source: Gail Blasser Riley, *Wah Ming Chang: Artist and Master of Special Effects*, pp. 78-79.

[178] Source: Sara McIntosh Wooten, *Oprah Winfrey: Talk Show Legend*, p. 39.

[179] Source: Jim Harmon, *The Great Radio Comedians*, p. 80.

[180] Source: Tom Feran and R.D. Heldenfels, *Ghoulardi*, p. 145.

[181] Source: Jack Mingo and Erin Barrett, *Lunchbox*, p. 9.

[182] Source: Toby Miller, *The Avengers*, pp. 26-27.

[183] Source: Ron "The Ghoul" Sweed and Mike Olszewski, *The Ghoul Scrapbook*, pp. 77, 79, 89.

[184] Source: Donald Brook, *Singers of Today*, pp. 129-130.

[185] Source: Gail Blasser Riley, *Wah Ming Chang: Artist and Master of Special Effects*, pp. 25, 27-28.

[186] Source: Art Linkletter, *Oops!*, p. 127.

[187] Source: Michael A. Schuman, *Will Smith: "I Like Blending a Message with Comedy,"* pp. 55-56.

[188] Source: Victor Borge and Robert Sherman, *My Favorite Comedies in Music*, p. 147.

[189] Source: Bill Adler, *Jewish Wit and Wisdom*, pp. 67-68.

[190] Source: a Lifetime *Intimate Portrait* program featuring Carol Burnett.

[191] Source: Herb Sanford, *Ladies and Gentlemen, The Garry Moore Show: Behind the Scenes When TV was New*, p. 101.

[192] Source: Joe Garner, *Stay Tuned: Television's Unforgettable Moments*, p. 5.

[193] Source: Stephen M. Silverman, *Funny Ladies*, p. 74.

[194] Source: Jay Leno, *Leading With My Chin*, p. 50.

[195] Source: Bill Adler, *The Letterman Wit: His Life and Humor*, p. 78.

[196] Source: Betty White, *Here We Go Again*, p. 55.

[197] Source: Rebecca Stefoff, *Mary Tyler Moore: The Woman Behind the Smile*, p. 58.

[198] Source: Sheldon Leonard, *And the Show Goes On*, pp. 146-147.

[199] Source: Robert Urban, "The Men of Sirius OutQ Radio: John McMullen." 17 May 2005 <http://www.afterelton.com/music/2005/5/sirius-mcmullen.html>.

[200] Source: Alexander Cho, "Passion Play." 30 October 2005 <http://www.georgetakei.com/frontiers/feature_second.html>.

[201] Source: John Javna, *The Best of TV Sitcoms*, p. 82.

[202] Source: Jimmy Crum and Carole Gerber, *How About That!*, pp. 178-179. Also: Jym Ganahl, speaking during a Channel 4 (Columbus, Ohio) newscast.

[203] Source: Carol Bauer Church, *Carol Burnett: Star of Comedy*, pp. 17-18.

[204] Source: Allan Neuwirth, *They'll Never Put That on the Air*, p. 148.

[205] Source: Keith Elliot Greenberg, *Charles, Burrows, and Charles: TV's Top Producers*, p. 77.

[206] Source: Phil Berger, *The Last Laugh*, p. 176.

[207] Source: Dave Rogers, *The Avengers*, p. 75.

[208] Source: Barry Took, *Comedy Greats*, p. 162.

[209] Source: Stephen E. Rubin, *The New Met in Profile*, p. 49.

[210] Source: Kermit Schafer, *Best of Bloopers*, p. 85.

[211] Source: Vince Waldron, *Classic Sitcoms*, p. 63.

[212] Source: Don Knotts, *Barney Fife and Other Characters I Have Known*, p. 189.

[213] Source: Robia LaMorte, "Christianity: Most Frequently Asked Questions." 26 November 2006 <http://www.robialamorte.com/main.html>.

[214] Source: an American Masters public TV program featuring Jack Paar.

[215] Source: James Hillis, "Gay Newsmen — A Clearer Picture." 13 May 2007 <http://www.afterelton.com/TV/2007/5/gaytvnewsmen>.

[216] Source: Candace Havens, *Joss Whedon: The Genius Behind Buffy*, pp. 34, 36.

[217] Source: Doreen Gonzales, *Madeleine L'Engle, Author of* A Wrinkle in Time, pp. 91, 95-96.

[218] Source: Duane Damon, *Headin' for Better Times*, p. 48.

[219] Source: Dave Rogers, *The Avengers Anew*, p. 74.

[220] Source: Patrick Macnee, *The Avengers and Me*, pp. 135-136.

[221] Source: Roger Ebert, "In Memory of Johnny Carson," *Chicago Sun-Times*, January 23, 2005.

[222] Source: Tom Feran and R.D. Heldenfels, *Ghoulardi*, pp. 31-32.

[223] Source: Kate Clinton, *Don't Get Me Started*, p. 117.

[224] Source: Amy Hollingsworth, *The Simple Faith of Mister Rogers*, p. 3.

[225] Source: Joey Green, *The Get Smart Handbook*, p. 17.

[226] Source: Ron "The Ghoul" Sweed and Mike Olszewski, *The Ghoul Scrapbook*, pp. 18-19.

[227] Source: Nancy Day, *Advertising: Information or Manipulation?*, pp. 34-35.

[228] Source: Peter Hay, *Canned Laughter*, p. 210.

[229] Source: H. Allen Smith, *Lost in the Horse Latitudes*, p. 184.

[230] Source: Nancy Cartwright, *My Life as a 10-Year-Old Boy*, pp. 180-181.

[231] Source: John and Kirsten Miller, *Legends 2*, p. 20.

[232] Source: Richard Kelly, *The Andy Griffith Show*, p. 118.

[233] Source: Spike Milligan, *Adolf Hitler: My Part in His Downfall*, p. 66.

[234] Source: Merrit Malloy and Marsha Rose, *Comedians' Quote Book*, p. 89.

[235] Source: Lawrence J. Epstein, *Mixed Nuts*, pp. 78-79.

[236] Source: Ron Smith, *Comic Support*, p. 85.

[237] Source: John Canemaker, *Tex Avery: The MGM Years, 1942-1955*, pp. 15, 18-19.

[238] Source: Alan Young, *Mr. Ed and Me*, p. 41.

[239] Source: Gerald Nachman, *Seriously Funny*, pp. 159-160.

[240] Source: Bradley Steffens and Robyn M. Weaver, *Cartoonists*, pp. 73-74.

[241] Source: Kathleen Tracy, *The Girl's Got Bite*, p. 97.

[242] Source: Henry Morgan, *Here's Morgan!*, p. 110.

[243] Source: Joe Garner, *Made You Laugh*, p. 113.

[244] Source: Stephen M. Silverman, *Funny Ladies*, p. 104.

[245] Source: Liza Donnelly, *Funny Ladies*, p. 114.

[246] Source: Jim Harmon, *The Great Radio Comedians*, p. 144.

[247] Source: David Morgan, *Monty Python Speaks*, pp. 213-214.

[248] Source: Ginny Weissman and Coyne Steven Sanders, *The Dick Van Dyke Show*, pp. 45-46.

[249] Source: Eddie Shapiro, "Desperate Dishing." 2 October 2005 <http://www2.out.com/detail.asp?id=13384>.

[250] Source: Sheldon Leonard, *And the Show Goes On*, pp. 112-113, 116.

www.ingramcontent.com/pod-product-compliance
Ingram Content Group UK Ltd.
Pitfield, Milton Keynes, MK11 3LW, UK
UKHW040030200726
13854UKWH00001B/457